Eden Falls

Deborah Holland Nunnery

Deborah Holland Nunnery

09-19-14

outskirtspress

DENVER, COLORADO

Outskirts Press, Inc.
http://www.outskirtspress.com

ISBN: 978-1-4787-3403-1

Outskirts Press and the "OP" logo are trademarks belonging to Outskirts Press, Inc.

PRINTED IN THE UNITED STATES OF AMERICA

> *"The mind is its own place and in itself can make a hell of heaven or a heaven of hell."*
>
> –Milton, *PARADISE LOST*

1.

October 31, 1998
Hilburn Sizemore

It was just a flicker, a nondescript image glancing through his peripheral vision, that gave warning he was about to fall asleep at the wheel. Without taking his eyes from the road, Hilburn reacted by slapping at the volume knob on the dashboard. It was an automatic move, perfected in the early days of delivering the *News Tribune* to the still-sleeping residents of rural Rose County. It sent the twang of bluegrass music from loud to blaring and proved as efficient a wakeup call as any windup alarm clock.

For twenty-plus years, it was here, near the end of his route, he always pulled over for a quick break. This was the very same place he enjoyed seeing steam rise from his thermos of black coffee as he took a long drag from the morning's first just-lit, non-filtered cigarette. That wonderful taste and aroma were the comforting habits that gave him the boost needed to help him wake up enough to finish his route and get home safely. Now, those vices were just memories and the blast of country hits from the local radio station had become his symbolic jolt of caffeine.

Last year, after chest pains ended in a frightening trip

to the emergency room at Rose County Medical Center, he made a promise to God to embrace a healthier lifestyle, a vow he was struggling with but was determined to keep. Now, Hilburn was a strict decaf drinker with a voracious cinnamon gum habit. That, along with an added dose of pure willpower from WOKZ-AM, kept him confident of his ability to stay awake and alert through a few more morning deliveries.

This newspaper route was as familiar as his own driveway, which meant it could turn dangerous, too, especially just before dawn when boredom and fatigue can sneak in and dull the senses. At this time of year, a slow-rolling fog could settle across the rural landscape, making it difficult to distinguish road from ditch. On this cool October morning, as he rounded the last curve of Old Post Road, his lack of sleep and craving for caffeine brought a new and frightening phenomena – hallucinations. Hilburn's growing fatigue, swirled and blended into the morning dew, creating a vortex of out of place images in front of the truck.

He slowed his vehicle to a crawl as the headlights made a glancing sweep across an image on the side of the road, grabbing his attention through a translucent veil of fog. A deer? Too small, he thought. A dog? Yes, a dog, maybe. All Hilburn saw when he squinted into the rearview mirror was an animal lying on the edge of the desolate farm road. That was all he could make out as the dim taillights attempted to pierce the hazy pre-dawn mist as it drifted across the road and seeped into the muddy landscape. Still trying to make sense of it all, Hilburn thought the strange-looking animal on the road resembled a person.

"What is that?" Hilburn asked himself as he looked in the mirror and saw it again. "What the hell?"

He craned his neck, stretching up close to the rear view mirror, struggling for a better view. His contortions, toes on the brake pedal and nose to the mirror, proved unsafe as his foot slipped from the brake, sending the truck lunging forward towards the opposite side of the road. A tire-screeching stop just short of a steep embankment left Hilburn's heart pounding and his hands trembling. This morning, it seemed fatigue and carelessness prevailed and, damned if he hadn't almost wrecked the truck.

"Crap!"

He flung open the glove box, groping and probing until he found the sworn-off pack of smokes and lighter, hidden for just such an emergency. WOKZ blared into the damp morning air from the truck perched on the edge of the ditch. His first taste of the taboo tobacco was stale but soothing and as the nicotine took effect, his racing pulse slowed and his shaking hands calmed. He inhaled deeply and prayed that God would forgive this one transgression. As he recuperated, the WOKZ announcer's voice blared into the morning air, reminding Hilburn of the time and season.

"It's six in the morning for all you early bird listeners out there. Coming up, the Sunday morning weather report but, first, don't forget tonight's Halloween party down at the armory! Make sure to bring the kiddies to the pumpkin-carving contest…and remember the curfew…nine o'clock sharp! Sheriff Sanders don't want any trouble like last year…"

That is when it hit him. Hilburn began to laugh, uncontrollably. His laughter rang across spent cornfields and echoed through empty tobacco barns along the final stretch of Old Post Road. The combination of fatigue and nicotine-induced euphoria did not help. Hilburn felt foolish but relieved.

Trick-or treat. That was it. This area had few creative outlets for bored teenagers and Halloween had become one of their favorite times to act out. This year, it seemed they had pulled a fine trick on the old paper man. He could just imagine the culprits hiding behind a nearby tree, laughing their asses off.

"Damn kids! I'm getting too old for this foolishness."

He tossed the half-smoked cigarette out the window and fumbled, once again, through the glove box, this time in search of a breath mint. Hilburn pulled the truck into gear and back onto the road, tires spinning dirt and spitting gravel. He was relieved to know this shift was nearly over.

When the sun began to peek over the horizon, it cast ominous shadows across the awakening landscape. Again, strange, out-of-place images started to catch Hilburn's eye. At first, barely visible through the darts of morning light that quickened across the asphalt, the images began to take shape. Women's clothing littered the roadside. A belt, muddy shoes, and tattered underwear were now clear, distinguishable objects that seemed to hint of a frightening crime scene ahead. This prank was becoming decidedly unfunny and Hilburn's patience was eroding. It was becoming obvious that these kids were copying something they saw on television.

What? Stealing pumpkins and soaping windows isn't a good enough prank these days? His left foot now rested securely against the brake pedal as the truck crept forward, the open window allowing a better view of the well-placed props scattered along the roadside. It was an amazing scene, very sophisticated, Hilburn thought. His emotions vacillated between anger at the vandalism and admiration at the artistic talent of these creative scoundrels.

"It's coming up on six-fifteen this Sunday morning..." The chipper voice of the WOKZ announcer reminded Hilburn that, as much as he would like to hang around to catch the clever kids who went to all this trouble for a silly Halloween prank, time is money and, after this exhausting paper route, he was ready to get home.

He floored it, speeding the last quarter mile towards the stop sign at the end of Old Post Road. He deliberately tried to keep his eyes straight ahead. He managed to ignore everything until he approached the next, truly disturbing sight. As before, he slowed the vehicle, inching along until his foot hit the brake, but harder this time, at the sight of a woman's purse, its contents strewn about. Something about this scene look real, not staged.

A chill, unrelated to the weather, crept up Hilburn's spine as he placed the truck in park, stepped out and began to trace the muddy trail back towards the curve. Even with a dense fog covering the now-completed sunrise, his vision was clear. He saw that what had looked like mud was blood and what he once was sure was a prank, was real.

His palpitations returned and he feared his heart would burst as he ran back to the truck and pulled the mobile phone from its dash-mounted cradle. He fumbled with the buttons but managed to call 911.

"I need a deputy, NOW." Hilburn had waited to get a

voice on the line before allowing himself to look back down the road toward the gruesome sight.

As the sun made its final push through thick fog, it sputtered in and out of the morning mist. Random darts of light flickered like a broken neon sign, flashing and shooting its angles back and forth, pointing to the spot where a woman lay, nude and lifeless. Her eyes were open as if she was still seeing her own murder, watching and reliving the exact moment someone threw her away like trash on the side of Old Post Road.

2.

March 8, 2005
North Carolina Central Prison
Abby Wilcox

A bby was nervous. Her calm, practiced façade began to wane long before the guard led her into the conference room. It started as soon as she drove through the entrance gate to North Carolina Central Prison in Raleigh. She jumped at an unexpected echo that rang out when the guard slammed the heavy door and another that sounded when she plopped her notebook on the table in the sparsely furnished room.

The calendar might read early spring but within the walls of Central Prison, it felt like winter. With every breath she took in, chilled air burned Abby's throat and each time she exhaled, a visible veil of fog hung briefly at eye level before wafting away towards the high ceiling. Two metal chairs, one on each side of the conference table, were not fashioned for comfort. They were heavy, purely utilitarian and looked as though they were made of steel. Lowering herself onto the chair, her muscles tensed in anticipation of the icy cold of the seat as it permeated her thin clothing. She braced for a sensation similar to touching one's tongue to a frozen flagpole. It was a silly thought, she knew, but a natural one given the stark environment. Yet, as is the case with most illogical thoughts and fears, it did not happen. Abby's ass did not freeze to the chair.

It took ten minutes for guards to bring the prisoner to the room. It seemed longer. Abby had rehearsed her interview questions for two days and feared another review might prove counterproductive so she chose not to open her notebook for now. To kill time, Abby studied the conference room itself, hoping that, later, she would be able to describe the sparsely furnished and jarringly cold space in detail. She counted the number of cinderblocks in the walls. She calculated sixteen blocks, herringboned to reach the ceiling, fourteen to the only source of natural light, a narrow egress window on the far wall. It allowed just enough daylight to cast shadows across the gray concrete floor. Polished to a high-gloss, the otherwise flawless floor had a massive eyebolt imbedded near the center. The other chair sat opposite the table, a chain's length away from the bolt.

Abby glanced at her watch. Just five minutes had passed.

She recognized this as a no-nonsense room, one created and decorated for short visits, a place, she imagined, intended for attorneys to meet with inmates between court appearances or, as in her case, for journalist/inmate interviews. This room was the judicial equivalent of purgatory, the place that separates the heaven of freedom from the hell of incarceration. Regardless of its use, the prison conference room adequately demonstrated the perfect example of form and function and that observation took up just two more minutes of time.

Abby was starting to question her sanity for coming, alone, to interview a death row prisoner. What could she hope to learn from this killer that she did not already know? Would confronting the person responsible for a heinous murder help Abby finish her book – the one with the twice-postponed deadline? Was this true investigative journalism or just a selfish search for personal peace? Perhaps Tom Kirby's obsession with Jessica Cline's murder had become her own. Abby's husband and coworkers thought so and often told her as much and, after ten minutes alone in an environment void of everything except introspection, she was tempted to agree.

The guard finally opened the door but did not assist the prisoner into the room. When inmate #23897 entered, Abby saw a heavy chain around his waist with links attached to his cuffed wrists and extending to shackles around his ankles. He gathered the long chain in his cuffed hands to walk without tripping, a method that only allowed slow, short steps. Watching him make halting, grotesque movements as he shuffled across the floor was a strange sight. Dragging his restraints, the prisoner managed to scoot himself onto the chair behind the table. He winced when the guard released the ankle cuffs, allowing a brief slack in the restraints before cuffing the prisoner's right ankle to the huge bolt in the floor. The clanging chains continued to ring throughout the, otherwise silent, space as he settled into his seat.

Four years ago, Abby watched officers lead him out of the Rose County Courthouse after his conviction of murder.

Today, he barely resembled the same man. Although she had been unsure of what to expect, she was surprised to see him so healthy and well groomed. She had to remind herself that, aside from concentrating on his legal appeals, physical fitness and grooming was all this man had to think about these days. It had been a week since he learned of her application to visit him and why. He could have refused to see her but waived that right. Now the two sat opposite the conference table with the clock ticking.

When he leaned back against the straight chair, his chains went silent and he stared at the opposite cinderblock wall. He did not look directly at Abby nor did he give any indication he remembered her. However, before she could speak, he proffered his first attempt to control the interview.

"So, you're writing a book about me. That's nice." His smug expression matched his clichéd tough-guy appearance, complete with shaved head and coffee-inked jailhouse tattoos. "Okay, so what do you want to know?"

"Well, you're partially right." Though shaken by his boldness, Abby refused to reveal she was intimidated. Neither would she let him manipulate the visit.

"I am writing a book – but not about you. I'm writing about Jessica Cline."

The prisoner tried to interrupt but Abby continued.

"And since you are the one person who knows the most about her, I want to hear what you have to say. After all, you know why she was murdered."

"Now, what makes you think that?" He leaned back, balancing the rear legs of the heavy chair as far back as his shackles would allow. He rocked back and forth with ease, looking quite comfortable.

She recognized this move to be a power play. It was his way of showing strength by demonstrating his ability to manipulate a thirty-pound straight chair into a recliner – in chains, no less. Abby's research had prepared her to expect such and her co-workers at the *Tribune* had told her to expect stunts like this one as well as his next move. They had told her that every prisoner quickly learned the art of staring at the ceiling, pretending to be deep in thought. "Just remember," said one co-worker, "That is when they were thinking up their next lie.

"For one thing, you've been convicted of murder. That, alone, makes you the only one in this room who has answers." Abby glared at the prisoner, though he had yet to look her in the eye.

"I-did-not-kill-Jessica Cline." He spat out the words, each one like a dagger intended to pierce Abby's emotions. It worked, too, but not for long.

Oh, no you don't, you bastard! Abby was livid and the clock ticked on. She had no time to listen to jailhouse denials, especially from a death row prisoner. Besides, no matter what trick he tried, Abby knew she was the smarter of the two.

"I don't have time for games, I want answers."

"Not 'til I know why you're here," he said. "I mean here – North Carolina. I thought you would have moved on by now. Got some big promotion with the FBI, maybe even with a big office in D.C." His lips curled into a surly smile.

"I have already told you all you need to know about me." Abby knew the real meaning behind his question. If not for

11

that telephone call from an old college roommate five years ago, Abby would still be in Atlanta, probably, still working for the FBI. Moreover, if anyone had told her, then, she would call Eden Falls, North Carolina home one day, she would have called them nuts.

"Say, how's your friend?" He looked at the ceiling as though trying to recall her name.

"Which friend?" She asked without looking at him. She sensed he was testing her.

"You know…the preacher's wife."

"Do you mean, Rachel? Rachel is fine." Abby slammed her notebook on the table and shot the prisoner as threatening a look as she could muster, "not that she's any of your business."

Abby took a long deep breath. Though anxious to hear the story from this creep's own mouth, she was unnerved and all she wanted to do right now was to reach the panic button on the wall and call for the guard. She wanted to get the hell away from this crazy man but just as she started to move, she noticed the clock over the door. She had only fifteen minutes left.

She thought back, recalling her Quantico training days and letting instinct and confidence take hold.

"Guess I was mistaken to think you would want your side of the story told. Clearly, I'm wasting my time." Abby shrugged and continued her move to the panic button knowing that most prisoners would never let her walk away. Most would kill all over again at the chance to have the last word. Abby turned her back to the prisoner, praying he could not detect her bluff nor her fear.

"Okay, okay." He took the bait and waved his free hand in a half-sincere surrender. "I'm only messing with you. I'll try to answer your questions – if I can."

Abby sat back down and tried to calm the butterflies that were having a party in her stomach. She opened the notebook then focused a non-blinking stare at the prisoner.

"Just tell me what you know." Her voice became assertive once again.

He hesitated before speaking. Was he trying to gather his thoughts or trying to sabotage the visit again by making up a better, more convincing lie? She could not tell but, by this time, it made no difference. She just wanted to hear something.

"If I tell you what I know, you have to promise to let the world know something about me. I may have hurt people, but I'm no monster." His heavy chair slammed onto the concrete floor and he leaned as far towards Abby as his chains would allow. "At least not as big a monster as others in Eden Falls."

Abby managed not to jump when the chair hit the floor and he lunged towards her, so close she could smell his bad breath. She did not react, waiting for him to continue.

"I can tell you things you don't know, but –". He gave a heavy sigh and for the first time allowed his eyes to meet hers. His voice became a whisper and, although Abby no longer felt the cold of the room, his stare gave her chills.

"I'll bet you a thousand dollars Jessica Cline's story is not what you think. It's probably worse – might even turn your stomach." The prisoner leaned back, once again turning his chair into a recliner. "Think you can handle it?" His surly

13

smile returned.

"Okay. Let's begin with the day of the murder." Abby began writing as she questioned the prisoner.

Note to self. No more eye contact.

3.

October 31, 1998

Omar Sanders

An extra hour or two of Sunday morning sleep was Sheriff Omar Sanders only plan for the morning. It was an infrequent luxury and one soon interrupted by a ringing phone then a pager. He ignored the phone but the pager buzzed once, then twice, then vibrated and danced across the bedside table until it hit the floor. Like a cat with nine lives and true to its settings, the pager resurrected every thirty seconds, demanding attention until Omar was fully awake. He was pissed at having to leave his comfortable bed but, by then, his sole motivation to get up was to find the little plastic nuisance and flush it down the toilet.

As past experience proved, weekend pages were, most often, unimportant, a thought that angered Omar when he looked at the clock and saw it was just ten minutes past six, barely daylight. Then he remembered.

"Aw, shit. It's Halloween."

He should have expected this weekend to bring trouble. Last year, the owner reported vandals had hit every car on the AutoMax lot. Eggs and chicken feathers, what a mess! It had taken hours to clean up all that crap, not to mention the time it took his men to round up the culprits—five bored teenagers full of Halloween mischief. That incident prompted this year's curfew order. From the sound of things, that had not helped much.

Numbers, 1-1-1, flashed, in red, across his pager. It was a private code set up between Omar and his lead dispatcher designed to separate serious calls from the mundane, the one that was meant to signal a real emergency. Omar could not help but wonder what kind of vandalism a few bored teens had committed, in the name of witchcraft, this year.

Less than ten minutes after the call, Omar was speeding towards Old Post Road. He wore a dirty wrinkled uniform, pulled from the laundry hamper and combed his thinning hair with the palm of his hand. Never a stickler for fashion, at this moment, appearance was of little importance to the Sheriff.

He pushed the cruiser way past the speed limit while calling dispatch for all available officers to meet him at the crime scene, instructing them to set up a roadblock at both entrances to Old Post Road in an effort to stave off the press.

Omar knew that reporters lived for this kind of story and, for now, he hoped the eighty miles per hour he was driving would beat the media hounds to the scene. If Hilburn Sizemore's call proved real, the first murder in Rose County in almost a century would prove a huge shock to the community. It would scare many locals but fear, of course, sells papers.

He could not help but wonder if he was speeding towards the work of a psychopath. If so, he had no idea what to expect since he had never, to his knowledge, been face-to-face with the work of a psychopath. He had to remind himself to calm down and not get ahead of things. After all, he was not sure if any of this really happened.

The sheriff held out hope that this was a sick Halloween prank until he got there. Upon arrival, it was clear that, this year, Omar faced a much bigger challenge than vandalized cars. He parked his cruiser well clear of the evidence field and grabbed his flashlight and gloves before joining Hilburn and first responders standing around the victim. He pulled on the latex gloves while he was walking and surveying what was now becoming a massive crime scene.

The yellow crime tape was beginning to sag under the weight of the morning dew, stretched beyond its limits around the acre-plus cornfield, littered with evidence. The victim was lying at the edge of the road. She appeared to have multiple stab wounds, too many to count from the way she lay. With her head in the mud, she was unrecognizable. Blood pooled around her head, making it impossible to tell her hair color. The only visible description was that she was tiny, no more than ninety pounds, Omar guessed.

He studied the knife wounds closely through the drying blood, making mental notes for the written reports to come. Experience told him one could determine origin of the victim's wounds, both direct and defensive, by the location and shape of the cuts. The slashes on the victim's legs, inflicted while she ran through the field and made in a downward direction, suggested a desperate struggle to escape her killer. Impossible, Omar concluded, since her efforts to fight back ended in near-decapitation from the blows to her neck and head.

Blood covered her entire body, except for her blue eyes, which were wide open and looked washed clean by her tears. Her haunting stare seemed frozen in horror, perhaps at the recognition of what was to come.

"I've never seen anything like this." Deputy James Wilcox pointed to the victim's lower extremities. "Even the soles of her feet are cut up."

Omar looked. "She was kicking at the knife after she fell. One thing about it, this little gal was a fighter to the end."

Sheriff and Deputy moved back to let the Medical Examiner take over.

"This death would have been slow and agonizing from the chase alone. But, it ended when the devil tried to cut her head off." Omar turned away from the Deputy before his emotions got the best of him.

"I've got to make some calls. James, you stay close and watch that no one contaminates anything here."

Omar managed to walk back to his squad car before shedding his first tear. He slid behind the wheel of the cruiser and locked the door, barricading himself from the commotion outside. Knowing his next step was one of the things he dreaded most, Omar sat alone for a while to gather his thoughts before placing a call to the State Bureau of Investigation. He had always been proud of his ability to handle problems in his county, no matter how serious, but this was different. This was big city crime, something that happened in New York or Charlotte, maybe Raleigh but for Rose County, this was an aberration. He swallowed hard and placed the call. The state boys would be here soon.

His emotions in check, Omar spoke to Hilburn Sizemore

who had just finished giving his statement. He sat on the bumper of his delivery truck, smoking a cigarette. In spite of that, Hilburn's hand still shook. As they chatted, a voice rose from the group of deputies standing near the body.

"Aw, I know this girl!" Someone said.

Omar rushed back to where the body lay and, within moments, realized that he and most everyone else in attendance knew her.

"Do not let the press in." Omar reminded his lead investigator as he looked around for Deputy James Wilcox. He and James would now make the most difficult visit of the day. They would be the ones to inform a nearby family that someone found their daughter's body on a country road less than a mile from her family's farm.

As the cruiser pulled away from Old Post Road, they met the *Tribune* reporters speeding towards them, horns blaring and lights flashing. They ignored attempts by reporters to stop them for a story. Must be losing their touch, Omar thought. He had beaten the media to the scene by a full thirty minutes and, while he was ahead of the game, he intended to stay that way.

The drive to the Cline farm was short, giving the sheriff little time to form a plan with his deputy.

"This is gonna' be tough, James." Omar pulled a toothpick from the half-empty box sitting on the console and inserted it between his lips. For the sheriff, toothpicks were a recent weight-loss trick, one designed to fool his mind into thinking he had just eaten. It was a good strategy but it had turned into a habit. While his forty-two inch waist had not shrunk, his craving and budget for mint-flavored toothpicks had clearly grown.

"There's a reason I asked you to come with me to do this." He rolled the toothpick around his mouth as he talked. "You're about the same age as the Cline kids and I thought you might have gone to school with some of them." Omar didn't appear to think that the sucking noise, made when he pulled the toothpick from his mouth, was the least bit offensive to those in his company.

"I know this family is a little strange, especially the father. Theo Cline is odd when sober and volatile when drunk and, even this early on a Sunday morning, sobriety among any of the Cline men is questionable." Omar plopped the toothpick back in his mouth.

"Yeah. I grew up with all three kids. When I was in the fifth grade, Nolan was two years ahead of me but by tenth grade, I had caught up with him. I remember he was a good artist but he quit and joined the Army. Wesley is my age but he dropped out of school about the same time, too. Next thing anyone knew, he was doing dope and stealing cars." James paused when he saw they were approaching the entrance to Cline Road.

Omar stopped the car to hear more. "What about Jessica?"

"Oh, yes, I know….knew… her. She was a couple years younger than me." James shook his head and added. "It's hard to realize that the happy little blonde haired girl I remember from grammar school is the mutilated corpse I just saw lying on the side of the road."

"Well, try to keep your emotions in check. We don't know how this family will react to this news." Omar said. "For that matter we don't know how much they know, either."

"Surely you don't think the family could have anything to do with something this horrible, do you?"

"I'm not saying anything of the sort, James but right now, you know we can't rule out anyone. Just follow my lead and be prepared for anything to happen."

Omar eased the cruiser up to the house. As he put the car in park, he added, "The only Cline I trust around here is Myra. She's a good woman…put up with abuse from Theo and those kids for a long time. I just hate for her to have to endure the news we have for her this time."

As the officers climbed the steps to the massive front porch, Omar thought he saw the shadow of someone peeking through an upstairs window. He rang the doorbell but got no response then opened the screen and banged on the massive front door. He could hear someone stirring inside.

"Stay alert, James."

The loud rap at the door startled Myra Cline from a hazy sleep. She fumbled for the handle on the side of the recliner and, after several tugs, released the chair into a sitting position, an act that exacerbated the pain in her arthritic fingers. It took extra effort to force the chair to an upright position, causing even more discomfort. She winced when a pain shot up her right arm like an electrical current, traveling to her neck, back down her spine then landing with a zap to her left foot. For Myra, it was an inconvenient malady but one she had learned to manage.

She often slept in the broken-down easy chair but usually avoided such a painful start to her day by practicing a

21

pattern of slow and measured moves. Nevertheless, the rude awakening that came at such an early hour on this Sunday morning caught her off guard. It startled her into moving too quickly, setting the pace for a day filled with the kind of pain this aging woman had never before experienced.

Now wide-awake, Myra moved towards the door but did not open it immediately, even after a second, more urgent, knock. Her hesitation had less to do with painful arthritis than her concern of who may be waiting outside. She peeked between the sheer curtains covering the wavy glass sidelights of the front door and sighed. When she saw the patrol car in the driveway, a familiar feeling of dread welled up and settled, like a poisonous knot deep in Myra's stomach. It was not the Sheriff's first visit to her door nor was it the first time she had been afraid to answer it. However, this was, the first time they had shown up before seven o'clock on a Sunday morning.

Myra stood still for a few seconds and leaned her head back towards the stairway, listening for sounds of snoring and taking a mental roll call of family members sleeping upstairs and down the hall. This had become her ritual, one played out whenever Myra's maternal instincts overruled her common sense. She opened the door, reassured that everyone was in bed, either asleep or passed out and braced herself for whatever was to come.

"Morning', Ma'am."

Sheriff Omar Sanders stood on the front porch with a polite half-smile on his face.

"Sorry to wake you so early but — can we come in?" He was already inside the door before Myra noticed Deputy

Wilcox. More than one deputy meant serious trouble, she thought, as she motioned them inside.

"What's wrong, Sheriff? All my kids are here. They are all upstairs—asleep. They're *all* asleep." As her voice trailed off, she worried, *but what have they done now?*

Sheriff Sanders had been to the Cline home on several occasions, often looking for either one of her trouble-prone, usually intoxicated, sons. The last time she remembered seeing Omar was about a month ago when he personally brought Jessica home, and told Myra he was giving her a break. Next time, he warned, he would arrest her for drunk and disorderly conduct. Myra would have been afraid he was there to make good on that promise if she was not certain, Jessie was upstairs, asleep in her bed. Still, she realized the serious nature of the call when Omar asked that Theo be present.

Theo Cline was already awake and stumbling into the den, zipping his pants as he walked and grumbling profanities about the early hour. Myra hated to get Theo involved. He usually made things worse. Sometimes, she found it easier to deal with bad news on her own since, most times, she could handle problems before Theo ever found out one existed. However, it was too late for that now, no matter the trouble.

"What in tarnation is all this?" Theo scowled at the deputies but motioned for them to sit.

"I'm afraid I have some bad news." Omar cleared his throat and continued. Ms. Cline, when was the last time you saw Jessica?"

"About twelve last night—when she came home. Why?

Should I wake her? She cannot be in any trouble this time. I saw her come in. I'll wake her up." Myra was still talking as she walked towards the hallway, her voice sounding purposely cheerful. She was relieved that, this time, her daughter could not be involved in whatever trouble had taken place.

"Ms. Cline, please come back and sit down. Jessie's not home."

Omar's use of her daughter's nickname was unusual. He had never done that before and, for some reason, it frightened Myra. What did he mean she was not home? She saw her come in. Her confusion kept her from hearing anything Omar said except, "...she was found about an hour ago."

"I'm sorry, Ma'am. Jessie's dead", he stated.

Myra stared at Omar in disbelief while Theo let out a thundering, "Oh, sweet Jesus!" before sinking into loud sobs. He buried his face in his sleeve and flung himself across the kitchen table.

The Sheriff reached out to take Myra's hand but she pulled away. *Don't touch me* she wanted to scream. She returned to the stairs to see the daughter's empty bed for herself. Saying nothing, walking slowly she returned to the den and her recliner.

"Ma'am, I know this is awful news to hear."

As Omar talked, Theo sat at the kitchen table, wailing loudly while Myra stared at Omar, tearless and unblinking. Her demeanor and voice, usually soft and sweet, began to grow loud, strong and demanding. "What happened?"

"Well, we don't really know for sure. Hilburn Sizemore found her about six this morning while he was delivering the paper on Post Road. We'll let you know more as soon as we

24

find out." His voice trailed off, becoming mere muffled background noise to Myra. She only heard part of what he was saying though none of it made sense. Just certain words or phrases were painfully clear. *We'll know more later...when they find out...medical examiner...anxious to get back to the crime scene...* What?

"Now, what time did you say you saw Jessie last night?" Omar asked Myra as he stroked her hand. However, right now, she would be neither comforted nor interrogated.

"But, what happened? You say she is...dead. What happened? Tell me. How?"

Myra choked back tears and pulled her hand away from Omar. Later, she told herself, she would have her own private breakdown, but not yet. She might be in shock from this news but she made herself clear, the Sheriff would answer some of her questions before she answered any of his.

Myra watched sons, Nolan and Wesley, as they came into the den, their faces acknowledging the fact that they had overheard the conversation. She knew they must be in shock at the news that their sister was dead. Myra hugged each of her boys and asked them to sit near her as she braced for the details to come.

"Ms. Myra, we don't know what, exactly, happened. Ah...she was attacked by somebody." He paused and Myra thought he appeared to be searching for words.

"The Medical Examiner will have to give us his report. But, for now," he continued, "we need to gather a few facts. Again, Ms. Myra, when did you say you last talked to Jessie? I know you don't want to talk right now but it's important to help us find whoever did this to your daughter."

She wondered if Omar was telling her all he knew but, for now, that did not matter. Myra decided she was not yet ready to hear the details. She would trust Sheriff Sanders to do his job. After all, she did not have much of a choice.

"Last night, she came in around midnight." Myra turned to stare out the window, blinking back tears. "I fell asleep." When she turned back to face Omar, her voice was calm and her words had regained their familiar softness. Her eyes glistened as she talked.

"I fell asleep," she repeated. "If I'd stayed awake, I would have heard...maybe, I would have heard her leave the house again. I could have stopped her...maybe. It's my fault."

Myra sobbed and pressed her face into the wing of Theo's old recliner that had become her sanctuary of late. Oversized and worn-out, it wrapped around and comforted her, the way Theo should do especially at a time like this.

However, Theo was inconsolable, too self-absorbed to make any move to reach out to his wife. Deputy Wilcox appeared to search the room, finally settling his focus on a box of tissues at Theo's elbow. He reached across the old man and handed the box to Myra.

"How about you and your boys, Mr. Cline — when did you last see Jessie?"

"Not seen her for days." Theo spoke between muffled sobs. "Myra, get me a glass of water...my heart hurts." He clutched his chest, breathing heavily. "If you fellows don't mind, can we do this later? I'm just too sick to talk right now. I think I'm gonna' pass...out."

Wilcox jumped up and reached for his radio to call emergency services but Omar motioned for him to sit back down. The Sheriff did not seem concerned about a pending heart attack by the elder Cline. He instructed James to get Theo a glass of water instead of the rescue squad, reminding him that Theo's pending heart attack would have been more convincing had he been clutching the left side of his chest instead of his right shoulder.

Omar stood.

"Mr. and Ms. Cline, we sure are sorry for your loss but we have to get back to our investigation. We will be in touch when we know more but, for now, someone needs to identify the…her body."

Myra sensed the urgency in Omar's voice but said nothing, waiting for Theo to respond but he just cried harder. She turned to Wesley and Nolan. The brothers became the ones to accompany the sheriff to identify their sister's body. When the deputies left, Myra turned to see Theo heading out the back door.

"Where are you going? We need to talk."

"I need a few minutes, Myra. I can't do this right now." Theo slammed the door on his way out.

"Good Lord, what happened to my baby? And, what am I supposed to do now?" Myra wondered aloud to an empty room. She slid back into her big old hand-me-down recliner and cried herself to sleep.

4.

November 12, 1998
Tom Kirby

"Evil has visited our community."
The minister's voice slowly hammered out each powerful word. Then he paused, making sure everyone within earshot had heard and grasped the importance of this five-word sentence. His somber tone and measured deliverance was appropriate for the occasion but served a dual purpose for Reverend Tom Kirby. As he preached his first, graveside, service at Bethel Baptist Church, all eyes were on him and he wanted to impress everyone in attendance. It was the first funeral he ever preached anywhere, a fact the congregation need not discover today but the added charge of preaching a funeral for a high profile murder victim was the true test for the young minister.

Tom Kirby's struggle to find positive qualities about the victim to include in her eulogy ended with little success. Even the girl's friends and family were not helpful. Knowing he would be remembered and judged by the words he said here today, Tom had resorted to pulling out notes from a long-ago seminary class, one intended to prepare him to conduct funerals for strangers. Meant to be a basic, one-size-fits-all eulogy, improvised but dignified, Tom knew that was not appropriate for this situation.

Tom wanted to find an impressive way to honor a now-infamous young woman he never met. It had not been easy but he pulled it off. Starting with the few good things he found out about Jessica Cline, he added his seminary training, his youthful charm, and threw in a little acting talent. After peppering his words with a little angst from his troubled past, he delivered a flawless performance to the somber audience. If his goal was to send this poor girl to heaven while gaining the respect of the congregation and the Deacon Board of Bethel Baptist Church, Tom Kirby had pulled it off.

Soon after the opening prayer, Tom relaxed as his confidence grew. He impressed the masses with his voice inflections and thought-provoking readings. He spoke flowery words of condolence to the family then ended the twenty-minute service by repeating his opening statement with a softer tone. His words were genuine but left a parting reminder of the unsolved murder.

"Yes friends, evil has visited our community. We do not know who took this young woman's life nor do we know why. However, it matters not for God knows and He will punish the guilty. So, friends, let us all keep Jessica Cline alive in our hearts and memory, knowing the peace she could not achieve on earth will be God's gift to her in heaven."

Since moving to Rose County six months before, Tom Kirby had faced an uphill battle of acceptance within this close-knit community. After Bethel's beloved minister of twenty-five years died, the Deacon Board hired Tom after just one visit. The young minister had charmed them with his youth, energy, and a promise to grow the congregation. As much as he had impressed the Board, Tom found himself smitten with picturesque little town of Eden Falls. The peaceful countryside was beautiful and reminded him of his grandparents' Georgia farm.

While expecting comparisons, at least for a while, to his predecessor, the ever-present scrutiny of the congregation and watchful eyes of the Deacon Board hindered Tom's search for acceptance in the community. It had been a slow journey, at best. He had overcome the sin of not being a local by reminding everyone that at least he was from the South. However, he could never overcome his biggest challenge, his age. After all, a twenty-nine year-old could not bring serious life experience to the job. Tom had promised to offset that flaw by growing the congregation along with church coffers by attracting younger, more affluent, worshipers. He had worked hard the past few months to make it happen.

Therefore, the high-profile funeral he preached today could make or break his career. One thing was for certain, the Deacon Board never expected to see so many people attend a singular function in the small cemetery of Bethel Baptist Church.

The weather on the day of Jessica Cline's funeral was unseasonably warm. Eighty degrees under a cloudless sky and blazing sun, it was humid, with little breeze. The funeral home's grave tent provided minimal shelter, barely enough to cover the grieving family members. Some in attendance were acquaintances and townsfolk, who ranged from the just plain curious to the gossip snobs who, in the past, would only acknowledge Jessica Cline with derogatory remarks or nasty name-calling. Others present included local law enforcement, SBI agents, and scores of media and newspaper reporters. It was not clear just why some people had come. Whether to soothe their conscience or gather fodder for the coming week's gossip, a sea of people found reason to crowd into the church cemetery that day.

Tom watched a news helicopter hover over the church grounds, filming the multitudes who gathered shoulder-to-shoulder in apparent loving support of the Cline family. He could envision the television announcer's voice-over of filmed coverage making a heart-wrenching story on the six o'clock news. Tom knew the footage would be misleading. In fact, most of the folks filmed were not leaning in to give support the grieving family. Instead, most were trying, in vain, to garner a bit of shade from the grave tent. It was clear, too, that empathy for Jessica Cline and her family went no further than the media's ability to manipulate a compelling story to boost their station's ratings.

Small town hypocrisy lingered in Reverend Kirby's mind as he watched the masses leave the gravesite in all directions, spilling across a large portion of the church cemetery. Attendees, both mourners and spectators, trampled centuries-old graves and tombstones on their way out. Any show of respect, spiritual or environmental, was, clearly, futile among a crowd of this size. Still, Tom could have never anticipated this scenario. All he could do was stand and watch, offering words of comfort to the unintentional vandals while, mentally, reviewing the past few days.

The Reverend never knew Jessica Cline, nor her family, except through the many Cline names etched into the largest stone in Bethel's cemetery but, by now, he felt as though he knew them all. Reading church history, Tom learned that, in 1880, Jonathan Cline donated fifteen acres of land to build a Baptist sanctuary. An inscription on a white marble monument centered in the church cemetery, immortalized him as church founder and community leader. It read:

Beneath lies Jonathan Cline,
Benefactor of this place of Worship
His beloved wife, Miranda,
And their issue
May God's Angels Protect
Bring them Peace
And Eternal rest

Tom discovered that Jonathan was Jessica's great-great-grandfather. There had been Cline family members listed on the church roster since its founding though the most recent generation seldom attended services. Regardless of having never met them in person, the Clines were important members of the congregation and the preacher did not hesitate when Deacon Smith called with news of the murder. Tom and Rachel would make the standard "Pastor and Wife" condolences call immediately after Bethel's Sunday morning worship service.

The Cline farm was no more than a five-minute drive from the church but, on the day of the murder, heavy traffic slowed the trip considerably. The congestion appeared to originate at the entrance to Cline Road where a long line of cars snaked along, trying to either turn into or out of the one-lane private road. A deputy directed traffic from the highway to the entrance to Cline Road.

The afternoon sun beat against the windshield, making it feel more like July than the first day of November. It was not a good day for a leisurely drive and when Rachel gave a forceful slap to the air conditioning button, Tom knew her frustration was growing. He worried she might not be prepared for this family visit and, fact was, neither was he. Dealing with a tragedy of this magnitude was new territory for them both.

"Look," Tom began. "I'm not sure what we're going to find here but, just so you know, we're only going to stay a few minutes. We will speak to the parents, offer condolences, and make sure they know how to reach us when they are ready to make funeral arrangements. I had no idea there would be so many people visiting the family so soon. Guess what they say is true. News travels fast, bad news, faster."

The role of preacher's wife was still new to Rachel and Tom realized she had already been out of her comfort zone on several occasions since moving here. Their college campus wedding had taken place less than a year before, just two weeks after graduation, him from seminary and Rachel from nursing school. The small ceremony had been the first step towards a future they had planned for four years, a plan that had always included a year of travel before settling down to start a family.

Rachel had voiced disappointed when Tom accepted the job in Eden Falls. He knew she wanted to see the world. She even talked of joining the Peace Corps or some other form of mission work. Once, when Tom reminded her of the hardship of living in a third world country, she had quipped that she loved the idea of being able to save lives while he saved souls. The last chapter of their well-planned future always ended with a move to a nice quiet rural area to raise a family. It had been a good plan but, somehow, just a few months into their marriage, the entire plan had reversed.

"Rachel..." He leaned over and kissed his wife. "You okay?"

"I'm fine, I'm fine! Let's get this over. It's hot as hell in this damned car!" She slapped at the air conditioner button again.

Tom winced then turned to his wife in preparation to repeat "the talk" for what seemed to be the millionth time.

"Alright...but please, Rachel, please...you know what I'm going to say. Promise you will not use that language around these folks. We don't want the first impression we leave with the Clines to be that the new preacher's wife has a foul mouth." Tom gave her a serious look for emphasis.

"Babe, I know my place." Rachel gave him a teasing grin back, adding in a barely audible voice, "Damn it, just shut up and drive."

They were finally close enough to turn onto Cline Road when the deputy threw up his hand to stop them. Tom showed his official identification and explained he was the family's pastor. The officer waived them through. Before pulling away, Tom asked the officer if there were many visitors with the family since the house was not visible from the road. His answer surprised Tom. No one was there except the Cline family and law enforcement. Clearly, the sea of cars causing all the traffic problems contained no one close enough to the family to actually stop and pay their respects.

How strange, Tom thought as he turned onto Cline Road.

Tom learned the quarter-mile driveway made for a bit of an adventure for first time visitors. Tall pines were interspersed with lush cedars, woven together with years of dense overgrowth. They lined both sides of the winding, one-lane and seemingly unending dirt path that led to the Cline home. Tree limbs and pine needles scraped the sides of the car as he maneuvered the hairpin curves. Tom wondered what he would do if he met a car coming out. His inability to see the road behind him, nor the Cline home ahead, made him wonder if it was possible to get lost on a one-lane path. Then, just as they rounded one more curve, the path opened to a huge front lawn and a stately house centered on the crest of a hill. The Clines let out a tandem sigh of relief.

"Wow!" Tom said, stunned by the view. "I certainly didn't expect this." He could tell the house had once been a beauty, reminiscent of a fine plantation left to decay.

"Damn! - Oops, sorry, Hon." Staring out the window, Rachel, too, seemed overcome by the surroundings and, though she seemed to try to stop her curse word, it had been too little, too late. "Tom, this place is gorgeous...or it could be, with a little work."

"Yeah, it's bound to be old. Antebellum, I'd say. Probably, the original home place from way back but it sure looks like there's been no upkeep since Sherman's army marched through this area." The preacher seemed suddenly oblivious to his wife's recurring bad habit.

"Just imagine raising a family in a fine old house like this." Rachel's preoccupation with the heat of the day seemed to have waned a bit, as well.

They sat in the idling car, admiring the architecture and discussing the millions it would probably take to restore the magnificent home to its original grandeur.

"Just look at those corbels holding up the porch, Rach. I bet each one would cost a couple of grand to make – if you could even get them made today."

Tom had not noticed the line of cars pulling in behind them until a deputy's car horn brought them back to the grim reality of the purpose of their visit. He pulled out of the way and parked, taking care to pick a spot where he could get out easily when it came time to leave. As amazing as the Cline homestead looked, he also felt a twinge of uneasiness with the place and wanted an easy exit.

Tom and Rachel welcomed the impromptu escort up the porch steps to meet the Clines, especially since Deputy James Wilcox was a member of Bethel Baptist Church.

"Sorry I didn't make it to services this morning, Preacher. We've been a little busy out here as you can see." James shook Tom's hand and reached over to open the screen door. "I'll make sure I get there next week." James knocked loudly on the door.

"I'm sure the Lord understands", Tom quipped nervously. He wanted to ask the deputy about the Cline's but the door opened before he had a chance. Deputy Wilcox introduced Tom and Rachel to Myra Cline who offered them a seat in the living room. The deputy excused himself, saying he had to speak with Wesley and Nolan, then left to join the Cline brothers in the backyard.

"No thank you, Ms. Cline." Tom responded to Myra's offer of a cup of coffee. "We are only here to offer our condolences. We are so very sorry to hear of your loss and to let you know that Rachel and I are here for you. So is the congregation."

As Tom waited for a response, he tried to read Myra's emotional state. He could not. In her eyes, he saw what he recognized as pain, but no tears. He saw what he perceived to be a state of shock, but no external expression of it.

After an awkward minute of silence, she responded. "Thank you Reverend Kirby. I'll get my husband."

Theo Cline came into the room. "Nice to meet you," was all he could get out before dissolving into tears.

With the proper expressions of sympathy, Rachel handed Myra a New Testament along with a book of inspirational poems. Tom made certain Theo knew how to contact him at the parsonage when they were ready to make funeral arrangements. There was very little conversation other than saying a prayer with the Clines. When Tom said "Amen", he opened his eyes to see James Wilcox standing in the hallway. He offered to walk Tom and Rachel to the door.

"As you can see, Preacher, we're still pretty early in our investigation." James sounded apologetic. "And, I guess it's clear that they are all having a hard time with this. I'll make sure the family calls you in a day or two to make the arrangements."

"Okay. Thanks, James. Let us know if we can do anything before then." Tom said as he started the car. The deputy nodded as Tom and Rachel pulled away from the yard and back through the winding maze-like driveway.

Tom was relieved that the same deputy was still directing traffic at the end of the driveway. It made the trip out to the main highway easier and the drive home much quicker. He sensed Rachel's eyes glancing back and forth at him as though she wanted to say something but was unsure as to what.

"Tom, do you find that family as strange as I do?" Rachel had found her voice. "Damn, they're weird. It was a little creepy back there." She rolled her eyes and gave a little shudder with her shoulders.

"Whatever I think, Rach, it is without the profanity." He was trying to take every opportunity to help his wife break her bad habit, for obvious reasons.

"I'm sure the Clines must be in shock. The mother showed no emotion – must not have hit her yet, and Mr. Cline — well, it's clear he's overcome with grief. He couldn't even talk without crying." Tom shook his head and added, "I'll bet, when all this sinks in they'll really need us."

"I guess you're right." Rachel's demeanor softened. "It is sad and I really do feel sorry for them but, you know who else I feel sorry for?" She turned to face her husband. "I feel sorry for you, too."

"Me? How so?"

"Baby, this is going to be a damn tough gig." Watching her husband shoot a look of disapproval her way, Rachel quickly corrected her statement. "I mean it will be a very difficult funeral assignment, dear."

Tom pulled the car into the parsonage driveway and stopped halfway. Rachel jumped out to unlock the front door while Tom drove into the garage. He knew his wife was right. This would be a tough funeral.

"Damn." Tom whispered to himself.

Prior to the funeral, local media filled the airwaves and

newsprint with unconfirmed speculation of the crime and gossip-laced stories of the victim. Knowing he had to comfort the grieving family at some point, Tom tried hard not to listen to the less-than-flattering stories that flooded in about the victim. He searched for positive facts, even anecdotal stories to present Jessica Cline in a softer light. Regardless of her reputation in the community, she deserved the respect of a dignified service. In addition, if the influence of a memorable eulogy encouraged the Cline family to become active members of Bethel once again, bringing their tithes and offerings with them, that would be a legitimate bonus the Deacon Board could not ignore.

It had taken three phone calls to schedule a meeting with Myra and Theo once the medical examiner released Jessica's body. He understood they were reluctant to answer the phone, certain that media was hounding them at all hours with stupid questions like, "How does it make you feel to lose a family member this way? Or, do you know who could have done this to your daughter?"

Tom heard it had become a nuisance. Just the day before, one obnoxious reporter was dumb enough to try to bully his way inside to interview Myra while deputies were changing shifts. Wesley Cline sent the reporter away with a broken nose and two black eyes. That incident prompted Sheriff Sanders to post two additional deputies at the driveway before a second killing in his county made headlines.

When Tom was finally able to schedule a family meeting, Myra was the only one to voice a desire about the funeral and she made it clear. She wanted her daughter's funeral to be a short graveside service.

"Ms. Cline, tell me about Jessie." The young minister used his most empathetic voice. "I want to memorialize your daughter with positive aspects of her life."

Myra summed up her child's life in just a few minutes, her monotone statement sounding rehearsed. Jessica Marie Cline was born September 23, 1968, the youngest of three children. Growing up, she was a happy child with an outgoing personality. She got good grades in school and liked to cook. After high school, she worked at a local diner and she planned to go to college someday.

Myra spoke with a flat affect. Her gaze remained fixed out the window, her voice bland and dispassionate. Clearly, someone had coached Myra for her role as family spokesperson. Her words held a rehearsed quality and Tom got the feeling she hid behind them like a protective barrier that prevented her from breaking down. How very odd, Tom thought. Surely, unashamedly, anyone would show raw emotion at a time like this. Apparently, the Clines took a very passive-aggressive approach to life. Still, Tom sensed that Myra was near breaking down, so he reached over and placed a comforting hand on her shoulder.

"Ms. Cline, what you tell us here today is not for anyone's ears by ours. It is just for me to get to know Jessica as a person since I never had the pleasure of meeting her."

Tom felt she was about to open up about her daughter but, before she could speak, Theo came into the room. He felt Myra's hand tense under his when Theo spoke.

"Myra, you'd best let me tell Reverend Tom the kind of funeral we want. Why don't you get me and the preacher a cup of coffee?" Then, turning to Rachel almost as I an afterthought, "How 'bout you, Ms. Kirby? Coffee?"

Before Myra could get out of her chair, Tom put out his hand to stop her. "No thank you, Mr. Cline. Please come sit by your wife and tell me about Jessica."

This must have taken Theo by surprise, for he complied and sat next to his wife. Then, as a tearless Myra continued to speak, Theo began, once again, to cry.

"Like I said," she continued, "Jessie worked at the diner and behaved like most other kids. She went on dates but never had a serious boyfriend. But then," Myra hesitated and glanced over at Theo, who did not return eye contact. "She ran away."

Myra's story continued, admitting how alcohol had been Jessica's downfall. She spent the final ten or twelve years of her life moving in and out of the family home. She would leave for weeks, sometimes months at a time, but always returned home. Myra said she would stay gone until she ran out of money or was on the outs with the friends and acquaintances who had been supplying her food and shelter.

Once, Myra said, Jessie went to California with "some people" then returned eighteen months later, unexpectedly. The pattern was always the same, each homecoming occurring at a low point in her life. Each time, she came back with a renewed determination to clean up her life and, always, promised to never leave home like that again.

"That's exactly what happened about six months ago", Myra explained. "She came back from a year-long stay in Florida...or South Carolina, or...somewhere." Myra could not remember but explained that was when Jessie had promised to give up drinking and drugs.

41

"It didn't take long to break that promise. I knew her old habits were back when she started leaving the house late at night. Several times, I watched her get into strangers' cars."

Myra did not know Jessie's friends by name and, by this time, she was too afraid to ask. Her disappearances, she admitted, usually ended hours or days later with Jessie coming through the door, stumbling drunk, or calling for someone to get her out of jail for public intoxication.

"Then, this time…this one time, I was sure she was okay. I was *sure*… but she wasn't." Myra's gaze trailed, once again, towards the window.

Tom took Rachel's hand and reached for Myra's with his other. Rachel followed Tom's lead and looked to Theo to join them. Instead, Theo stood up and stumbled from the room. The distraught father appeared overcome with grief, unable to hear any more.

"I'm sorry for that." Myra nodded towards the retreating Theo. "He's just so upset."

Tom reassured Myra that he understood then, holding the two women's hands, said a short prayer. Afterwards, he asked Myra what kind of service the family would like. Tom watched Myra make certain Theo was out of earshot before she answered. Then, turning to face him, Myra made eye contact for the first time that day.

"A quick one", was her, barely audible, response. "I just want it to be over."

When Tom left the Cline home for the second time, he knew little more about the deceased than when he made the first visit. He left, still searching for a positive side to this young woman's life.

Rachel tried to reassure and remind Tom that he would do a fine job. She reminded him he was a good minister. Still, Tom felt a strong obligation to deliver this particular eulogy. He knew he would wrestle with every word he prepared. Now, more than before meeting her family, Tom saw the victim as a true lost soul. Her funeral would be the last chance for anyone to say good things about her. His fear was, after her burial, the story would no longer be about the victim, but her notoriety. Furthermore, for some reason, Tom was starting to feel a strong connection to Jessica Cline.

Yes, the past week had been a wild ride and now, Reverend Kirby ended the graveside service by repeating his opening remarks, hoping his words were effective. The throngs dispersed at last and Tom walked back through the cemetery. He watched the funeral home workers load folding chairs and artificial turf into the truck and pull away from the churchyard. For the first time since early morning, the graveyard was quiet. The masses were gone, leaving the dead to rest in peace, once again.

None of those present that day would know that Bethel Cemetery, that little city of eternal rest behind the country church, would be the only place in Rose County to remain calm and peaceful for many months to come. Rose County was proud of its claim to quiet living, a safe place where nothing bad ever happens. Eden Falls was the county seat and town leaders boasted, via the billboard on Highway 37 "Visit Eden Falls, a paradise second only to the Garden of Eden".

The thought of anyone in this community harboring evil deeds was unconscionable and most of the mourners in attendance that day would walk away, believing the murder of Jessica Cline a fluke. They would envision her murder as a random act committed by a transient killer, moving through Rose County like a fast rolling storm, striking with lightning speed, only those deserving of God's wrath. Many would compare this murder to a swift summer storm, believing that, regardless of the damage, the sun would return and life would go on. In Eden Falls, evil could not survive. They would force it out of town and forget it.

5.

February 8, 1999
Myra Cline

After hanging the Monday morning laundry out to dry, Myra had time to sit down and rest a bit while she opened the mail. The letter from the Rose County Sheriff's Department took precedence over the junk mail and bills that sat in a growing but unacknowledged pile on the hall table. The now-familiar envelope with its government seal stamped prominently in the left corner no longer made her heart pound with expectations. Still, this time there might be new information.

Until recently, the deputies stopped by every week, just to let the Clines know they were still investigating, but had nothing new to share about her daughter's murder. It was a courtesy, not particularly necessary but comforting, still. That visit was something they had not done lately. She understood. It must be hard to try figure out how to say the same thing more than a dozen or so ways. *No leads... we have nothing new ... we just don't know,* and so on.

By now, she had memorized the theory of the stranger passing through Rose County, the now-infamous psychopath who, unnoticed, stalked the area for days in search of the perfect victim. Moreover, Jessica was the one unfortunate soul he could lure from her bed and into an open field late at night. Everyone said she was easy prey, a loner not missed right away. Myra listened to their story of the psychopath every time the deputies came by. They always reminded her that the killer probably disappeared to somewhere far off and untouchable. Authorities might never find him.

The deputies always ended their visit with an apology as if saying they were sorry was the only salve they had to sooth her wounded heart. It did, sort of, because the deputies never acted as if they had heard the awful things said about Jessica, and she appreciated that. Though not told things directly, the gossip and nasty rumors easily found their way down the winding Cline Road and directly to the grieving mother. However, they never came from law enforcement. The deputies showed her respect and never repeated the awful news of the grapevine that Jessica's lifestyle had caused her death.

Myra's own sisters had no problem telling her such things. They never found time to visit but managed the call every night to fill her full of the day's gossip. They were trying to be helpful, she knew, but they could never understand how much it hurt to hear such terrible things.

Today's official letter, like all those before, stated that there were no new leads in the investigation. As she re-read the letter, her heart searching for information that her mind knew was not there, a light tapping sound on the tin roof caught her attention. She pulled herself up, knowing what she would see, even before reaching the window. Sure enough, after spending two hours washing clothes that now hung on four wire lines slung low with the weight of heavy denim jeans and cotton work shirts, a steady rainfall had set in to ruin all her work. Laundry was the chore Myra hated most but was resolved to do. Three men could sure dirty up some clothes.

She knew that her boys, as she called Noland and Wes, would need those clean clothes the following week. If they were not clean and pressed by Monday morning, they would have another reason not to work. In addition, if they could not work they would have an excuse to get drunk, not that they need an excuse. It seemed Myra's job these days was to make sure her boys had clean clothes and full stomachs. That was her contribution to helping keep them employed and sober.

The knots that surrounded the joints of Myra's, otherwise, thin fingers always got in the way of simple tasks. This time they slowed the process of tying the plastic rain bonnet under her chin as she watched the soft rain turn into a heavy shower.

Looking out the open kitchen door, she saw Theo's truck pull into the yard. She yelled for him to help her pull the clothes from the line, but she could tell, he could not hear her through what had quickly become a thundering downpour. He bounded from the truck, up the porch steps and rushed past Myra, shedding his clothes as soon as he was inside. Theo's muddy garments, including shoes and socks, piled on the floor as he disrobed with lightning speed. He was down to his underwear before he realized that his semi-fresh pants and shirt that always hung behind the door were missing.

"Dammit, Myra! Where're my clothes?"

Only then, did he turn to see that his wife of fifty-plus

years had ignored him and was running outside, slamming the screen door behind her.

"Where the hell are you goin'…don't you see it's rainin'? And…dammit, Myra! Where the hell are my clothes?"

She did not bother to answer. Myra had given up, long ago, trying to reason with Theo. Furthermore, when folks asked why she never stood up to him, she thought that question just as crazy as Theo's behavior. Myra now made it a practice not to waste time trying to reason with fools.

She worked fast, trying to salvage as much of the laundry from the line as possible, making sure that Theo's clothes were the first ones retrieved. If she hung them over the bathtub, she figured they should be dry by late this evening, As she worked, she noticed her husband standing at the back door wearing an old pair of pants and a shirt he must have found in a remote corner of the closet. She could only imagine the odor they emitted after exposure to the damp outside air and was surprised that he could stand to wear them. She was surprised, too, when he yelled out to ask if she needed his help. Myra shook her head yes, pleased at his offer.

Theo dashed from the house, ran past the clothesline and straight to his truck where he pulled something from the front seat and returned to his wife's side. He opened a large black umbrella and held it, with both hands, over his wife's head. He was impatient but hovered and waited until she had pulled down the last of the jeans. Theo walked next to Myra, shielding her from the rain with his huge umbrella and watching her drag the basket of clothes into the house. She had decided to leave the remaining soaked garments for eventual sunshine.

Once inside, Theo sank into his recliner complaining that his rheumatism would surely "give him a fit" after that painful experience. Myra was only half-listening as she hung the clothes across the shower rod and reminded herself that her husband was not, altogether, a bad man. At least, he held the umbrella for her.

The rain tapered off as a late afternoon sun peeked around the clouds. Myra watched the remaining clothes that hung, dripping, on the line and anticipated a sunny tomorrow.

She set the table for supper even though she knew that, when she was finished, her family would grab a plate of food and migrate to the den, leaving her to dine, alone, at the kitchen table. She could not remember when this became a ritual but it had become one that she did not mind so much now. This dining arrangement kept her from losing her appetite, which always happened when watching the poor table manners of the men in her family. Of more importance, it made Jessie's absence less noticeable. Anything that kept them from having to acknowledge the obvious was best, Myra thought.

It had been nearly four months since the murder, enough time for it to be real but not long enough to talk about it with Theo and the boys. Just thinking of Jessie made Myra cry, especially if she allowed herself to remember the little blonde three or four year-old, the baby girl she loved so much.

Now unable to remember the exact age the sweet little girl turned into a wayward youngster, to Myra, it seemed to have happened in an instant. Jessie turned from a happy, trusting child into a brooding, troubled teen and no one understood why. Myra had blinked and, when she looked again, the bright smiling eyes of her youngest child had turned dark and empty. It was as though something had reached inside her and snatched out Jessie's soul.

Myra feared she had started to run with a wild crowd and she tried to talk to her daughter about it. She even tried to get her to talk to the preacher. Jessie refused to speak with Preacher Hill who was elderly and set in his ways. Maybe, she would have listened to someone kind and understanding, like Reverend Kirby. Nevertheless, there was no sense worrying about that now. Reverend Kirby was not here then and Jessie's not here now.

After supper, Myra remembered the mail that had come from the Sheriff's Department. She was about to show it to Theo when she realized he was sound asleep in his recliner. Had she been ready for an argument, she would have awakened him, shown him the letter and begged him to go into town the next morning to demand they look harder for their daughter's killer. Had she not been too tired to endure Theo's fury, she would have awakened him and demanded he talk to the authorities about the people who caused Jessie's death, the ones who had taken her happiness, her soul and, finally, her life. However, Myra did not have the energy, nor the will, to endure Theo's wrath; best let sleeping dogs lie.

The night ended as most had for the past six months, with Myra easing into her recliner in the den. She said a silent prayer for God to guide someone to her child's killer. Then, she prayed for her own soul. Maybe God would forgive her for what she wanted to do to the person who killed her baby.

Wesley's anger grew by the minute. This was often his state of mind the last few days of the month. That was when money and booze were in short supply in the Cline family.

He slapped at the calendar, tearing it from the flimsy hook holding it to the kitchen wall. "Shit…three more days until the checks come. Damn Social Services! Why don't they just send enough money to last the whole month?" He kicked the calendar across the floor. "Assholes" he added before storming out of the house.

There had already been trouble that morning when Wesley and Nolan had tried to wake Theo from a sound sleep. The brothers wanted money and a ride to the local bootlegger's house to buy a little something to stave off DT's. Theo refused their request by way of a middle finger gesture before rolling over on the couch and resuming a loud snore. Unable to roust Theo, the brothers began to curse and fight each other while Myra expressed her disapproval in her usual passive-aggressive way. She swept the kitchen floor in silence.

Breaking away from the fight, Wesley shoved Nolan back inside the house and slammed the kitchen door to get away from him. This scenario, or some variation of it, had become commonplace, almost ritualistic, near the end of each month. Seems the older they got the more the brothers fought. Even to Wesley, that felt backwards. Sibling rivalry should lessen in adulthood. Right?

His childhood memories, full of fistfights with his brother, rarely included intervention from Theo or Myra. Bigger and stronger, Nolan was always the victor. Wesley could not remember a single time he came through one of their tangles uninjured.

His only reprieve came with Nolan's army enlistment in 1990. Then, for five years, Wesley reaped the benefits of being Myra's son — for a while her only son. That was the first time Myra ever doted on Wesley, cooking his favorite meals and giving him extra money without him even having to ask. However, his mother's gesture never seemed genuine. Wesley wondered whether Myra was afraid that he, too, would enlist and leave her alone with Theo. Perhaps, she worried that Jessica would show back up again, in trouble, as usual; trouble she would have to handle alone. Myra's reason was unclear. Whatever it was, Wesley knew he was just a temporary substitute for his brother. The proof came each night at six o'clock when Myra's attention turned to television and the evening news reports of Operation Desert Storm. She would sit close to the screen and scour the news reports as if she might actually see Nolan wave to her from the grainy footage of the troops. Crazy woman, Wesley thought.

At times, Wesley wished his brother would die over there and he was not ashamed to admit that. After all, no one would miss him, except for Myra and, Wesley was sure she would get over it eventually. Fact was Nolan was mean. He was a bully and always had been. Serving two back-to-back combat tours made Nolan's chances of getting killed a good bet. On the other hand, maybe being shot by a pissed off fellow soldier was even more likely. Either way, Nolan's demise would sure solve some problems for Wesley, such as his plan to leverage a sizeable tab at Bootlegger Pop's by being the brother of a dead war hero. All those plans ended

52

with Nolan's return. That is when he had to rethink how he would handle his brother's homecoming since being in a war zone for that long was bound to make him meaner. Nolan came back a changed man, all right but not the way Wesley expected.

Nolan had always looked older than his age but now, he looked older than Theo did. He was thin and in the past two years, his skin had a taken on a strange orange tint, cracked, wrinkled, and baked to toast in the desert sun. The whites of his eyes had turned yellow and his formerly dark hair had turned white. When he spoke, which he rarely did, his voice was raspy and his words always ended with a cough that sounded like he was trying to expel desert dust. Sometimes he coughed so hard it sounded like he was trying to cough up a camel. It looked, to Wes, like he had left an entire Nolan somewhere in that Persian Gulf desert, returning with little more than a shell of his former self.

Myra had fed and babied Nolan for months to get him re-nourished but, hard as she tried, she could not fix whatever part of her favorite son was broken. Wes could tell that Nolan was mentally slower than before and, somehow knew that his brother would never be the bully he remembered. He had lost his edge.

Wesley never thought he would feel sorry for Nolan but now, he rather pitied him. After all, fighting was the only skill Nolan had ever developed but since his return home, his appetite for mayhem and local terrorism had dissipated. However, he had retained his non-discerning appetite for booze. These days, Nolan would drink anything as long as it was no farther than an arms-length from the couch. He was not motivated to get up unless necessary. It was doubtful, he thought, Nolan would move for a house fire unless it started under the couch.

Wes could tell from Myra's actions that she was happy to have her favorite son home from the war and excused his every shortcoming. She blamed Nolan's lack of motivation on the army, claiming they abused him by making him serve double the time. She refused to believe that Nolan volunteered for that second tour and requested a third.

"He was brave enough to serve his country valiantly, he should be allowed to do anything he wants", Myra would say. Wesley watched his mom encourage Nolan to paint again. Everyone remembered his talent but Wesley could tell, since coming home, his brother was only motivated to drink and hold down the couch. No one else seemed to notice.

"Leave him alone. He is a decorated Veteran, after all", Myra said, repeatedly.

One would think that Nolan had saved America from the terrorists single-handedly. Wesley knew his mother would never realize it was he who kept the farm intact for five years while Nolan was in the army, Jessica walked the streets in strange cites, Theo was – wherever Theo goes, and Myra sat staring at the twenty-four hour news channel on television.

When Wesley began to sweat profusely, his worries turned from his crazy brother to the task of finding Theo's stash of liquor or, maybe something of value to pawn for liquor and a ride to bootlegger Pop's. He walked fast towards the hog pen; a dump area, area set a short distance behind the house, overgrown with trash and no longer fit to house hogs. He kept glancing back to make sure Nolan was not behind him. That, Wes thought, was what set him apart from his older brother.

"Damned if I'm gonna' just lie on the couch and die. Who's motivated now Ma?" Well out of earshot, Wesley broke into a sprint.

Theo's truck was a fortress, always locked, entry forbidden to everyone but Theo. The rusted out clunker sat near the edge of the woods just far enough away from the house to blend in and become a part of the over-grown cornfield that divided the home place from the fifteen-plus acres of dense, virgin woodland. While easily seen from the kitchen window, it was not visible from the road or driveway.

Wes had overheard Myra's frequent complaints to Theo about the growing junk pile near the house. Though hidden by head-high weeds, she had fussed about cleaning up the acre of discarded appliances, tires and garbage. Not that she had seen it up close, mind you. Wesley knew she was not brave enough to venture into the area that the whole family called the hog pen. Theo had told her the area was dangerous. Besides being rat-infested, there were snakes breeding among the piles of tires, car parts and old appliances that had found their final resting place in the bowels of the hog pen. He knew she had no desire to fight rats the size of small dogs, or worse still, take on the snakes, even the likely non-poisonous kind that made their home deep within all that garbage.

Over the years, keeping the area in squalor became a ploy used by Theo to keep prying eyes away and in a family whose practice was to avoid conversation about everything; its secrecy was easily preserved. Wesley sometimes wondered at how odd it was that three men with nothing in common but blood would hold such a place sacred.

He was not sure what year Theo found that specific spot in the hog pen, behind the shed, a safe place to stash his old truck. Rust and mud now covered its surface, which helped it blend into the landscape, creating an ingenious camouflage. Tinted windows and locked doors made a clever repository for old unpaid bills, near-empty liquor bottles, and the remnants of sick family secrets. Since Myra would never venture near the area, Wesley knew the locked doors were to keep him out, and Nolan, and anyone else who might be snooping around. It was the first vehicle Theo ever bought new, his first major purchase and the one possession he would never give up. Moreover, it was booby-trapped — at least that was what Theo had told them. That story, along with death threats and lesser intimidation, kept everyone away from his truck so effectively that Theo seemed to no longer worry about whatever he had stashed under the front seat of his special hiding place.

Wesley and Nolan did not care they were banned from that old truck. There were plenty of other hiding places around the hog pen that the Cline brothers could hide stolen goods they often "found". Pop would always take their finds in trade for liquor. As far as Wesley was concerned, Theo could have that old piece-of-shit truck. Wesley was good at finding Theo's other forgotten hiding places but, before he went into full blown DT's, all bets on the safety of Theo's locked up truck would be off.

Wesley walked around the old Ford, trying hard to see inside the dirty, tinted windows. He leaned against it and slid down bedside the front passenger door, landing in a squatting position. As he tried to gather energy enough to break into Theo's truck window, a glint of light caught his eye. He traced it to a bottle hidden behind the front tire on the passenger side. A bottle of Ancient Age whiskey held at least two good swigs of booze. Wesley turned it up and drained the contents, barely tasting the warm liquid but soon feeling its affect.

Allowing the booze to hit its mark somewhere between his tongue and stomach, Wesley stumbled back to the house. By the time he hit the porch, he was feeling better. He waved to Myra as he floated through the kitchen and high-fived a semi-alert Nolan.

By the time Theo got home, Wesley was in his room, mellowed out on rock and roll. He watched from the window as his father walked up the steps.

"Your old piece-of-shit truck dodged a bullet today, Ole Man!" Wesley shouted to his father. His words, muffled by the closed window, meant Theo and his old truck would live to see another day.

Wesley closed his eyes and fell asleep to an honored lullaby, "Junk Head" by Alice in Chains.

"Damn it, Wesley!" The screen door banged against Nolan's forehead from the force of his brother's hand, sending him stumbling backwards, inside the kitchen, the dinette chair catching his fall. Without taking his eyes off Wesley, who was running down the drive away from the house, Nolan reached back to find the chrome frame of the chair. His fingers traced the curve of the cool metal to the cushioned vinyl seat. He plopped down and rubbed the knot that had started growing between his eyes. He could not understand. When had his little brother become stronger than he was?

"I do wish you boys would stop this foolishness." Myra slapped a cold cloth against Nolan's forehead and picked up his limp right hand to hold it in place. She shook her head as she returned to her dishwashing. "I thought you two would grow up one day. You'd think you were ten years old instead of forty."

Once upon a time, Nolan, too, was anxious to become an adult. He genuinely wanted to grow up and get away from Eden Falls. However, that was long ago – before Desert Storm – before his sister's murder.

Nolan remembered the day his parents brought his little brother home from the hospital, all red-faced and squirmy. Even at fifteen months of age, Nolan was sure his parents brought Wesley home, solely, to usurp his place in the family. Each time he tried to pat Wesley's little face, just to see what it felt like, his mother would push his hand away. That was when Nolan first sensed he was no longer special in his mother's eyes and, with Wesley's every cry; he became more certain of it. Nolan fought with Wesley for Myra's attention and affection from the beginning.

As they grew, Theo was never concerned about the boys' squabbles, calling it nothing more than sibling rivalry. It mattered little that they were small children. Theo demanded they "fight it out in the yard like men". So, they did – often. Nolan and Wesley's brawls were loud, bloody, and daily and Myra ignored them, retreating, instead to the safe haven of her kitchen where the volume of the tiny counter-top television drowned out the sounds of her sons' fights. Theo, however, took joy in seeing his boys beat the crap out of each other. His reward to the winner was to chastise and belittle the loser. With his year-plus head start of growth over Wesley, Nolan quickly became the favored winner over his little brother. However, that was a short-lived advantage. When the contest was no longer close, Theo lost interest. It was clear Nolan's growth spurt, at age ten, gave him the edge, so his only choice was to pretend to like his little broth-er. After all, Nolan thought, short of someone killing him, Wesley was not going away any time soon.

When little sister, Jessica, came along, Nolan had already given up on being the parental favorite. Wesley was the cute child, the knee baby who could get away with most anything and Jessie was the princess. She need only smile at her par-ents to inherit the world. All Nolan had going for him was that he was the oldest and biggest. He was a bully. Myra and Theo knew that, so they gave him a job.

At age ten, Nolan became the babysitter and unpaid bodyguard who, quickly, learned to be a double agent. Nolan protected his siblings when his parents were looking but, out of sight, he was their tormentor.

"Nolan…Nolan!" Theo's booming voice could startle him from a deep sleep quicker than the loudest alarm clock Sears sold. Deep and commanding, it traveled up the stairwell as if the devil himself had shouted directly from hell. "Get down here and help everybody get ready for school. If ya'll miss that damned bus, you'll just have to stay home. I ain't got time to haul your lazy asses to that school house today!"

"Coming," Nolan yelled back. "You asshole," he added under his breath. Nolan loved to repeat Theo's own curse words. Even whispered, it was sweet revenge and made Nolan feel like a grown-up or, at least, older than ten.

Thus, a typical day began to repeat for Nolan, eight year-old Wesley, and six year-old Jessica. The tension-filled morning lasted until the three boarded the safety of the school bus where Nolan could relax and enjoy the ride.

He liked school; some subjects more than other ones, some days more than others. Wednesdays were good. That was art class day. Nolan loved art so he always looked forward to Wednesdays. As he climbed the steps to board the bus, he recited as his foot hit each step, "I…love…Wednesdays." He smiled up at the bus driver.

"Will you hurry up, kid?" The driver was unimpressed and, obviously, not such a fan of Wednesdays. Nolan took his favorite seat on the back row and pulled out his binder.

From the back seat, Nolan could keep an eye on his siblings and he could draw for the entire thirty-minute ride, without snooping eyes over his shoulder. Sometimes, he managed to complete a picture before the bus pulled into the school lot even allowing for interruptions by having to erase mistakes caused by bumpy roads and jerky gearshift changes by the driver. Sometimes, he finished by being the first one in the room, taking his seat just before the bell rang and, usually, he had time to slide it into his notebook before the teacher ever noticed.

"But, Ms. Carson…it's not finished yet." His teacher had taken him by surprise and, before he felt her presence over his shoulder, Nolan found himself handing her the unfinished picture and an awkward apology.

"Oh, Nolan…" The teacher gave a short gasp as she held the drawing up to the light. "It's beautiful."

She studied the pencil drawing of a horse running across a pasture. She glanced back and forth between the picture and the student, comparing and trying to reconcile the two. She held a surprised smile and somehow Nolan knew she was sincerely pleased with his work. His fourth grade teacher had discovered Nolan's talent and praised him for it. It was the first spark of encouragement Nolan had ever felt in his short life.

Ms. Carson sent a note home to Theo and Myra that afternoon. It was sealed and Nolan knew better than to try to open it. Theo was keen to that trick. Besides, this time Nolan was not worried about the content of the note. This time, it was praise rather than a suggestion of punishment for some bad act.

That evening at dinner, he held out the note to Myra. "Ms. Carson wanted me to give you this." He had trouble hiding his excitement.

"What in the world?" Myra asked as she wiped her hands on her apron. Before she could take the note, Theo reached over the stew pot and grabbed it

"What the hell trouble have you got into now, boy?"

"Nothing, Pa." Nolan should have known his father would have to read it first. Theo tore into the envelope, read it to himself and tossed the paper on the table. He turned toward Nolan and shook his head.

"What did it say?" Nolan waited for a response from

61

his father who walked, without a word, into the den where he turned on the television and began flipping through the channels.

Myra picked up the note and began to read it aloud.

"I am pleased to inform you that Nolan has excelled in art class. His pencil drawings show great promise and I have recommended him for our new art program that begins after we return from Christmas break. I have enclosed a permission slip for you to sign, allowing him to stay after school two days a week to meet with Charles Simmons, Rose County's Artist-in-Residence. If you have questions, please contact me. Evelyn Carson, Eden Falls Elementary School."

"How, nice!" Myra leaned over, kissed her boy on the cheek, and added, "I'm so proud of you!"

"Theo, did you read this?" She had followed her husband into the den, shaking the paper in his face.

"'Course, I saw it. I read it before you." Theo pretended to watch the news, trying.to ignore his wife.

"Well, aren't you going to tell your son how proud you are of him?"

"Hell, Myra, he knows I'm proud." He leaned around Myra, who stood, arms crossed and blocking his view of the television, and yelled back to the kitchen. "You know I'm proud of you, don't you, boy?"

Theo grabbed Myra's arm and pulled her face close to his. "I won't let that school teacher put fancy ideas in that boy's head. I won't have it!" He released her arm but added, "drawin' pictures is sissy. There ain't never been a sissy man in the Cline family and I ain't about to let any son of mine turn into one."

When Myra turned to leave, Theo added, "Myra, You send that note back and tell that teacher, no thank you. That's how homos get started, you know."

Myra walked back into the kitchen to find Nolan listening from behind the kitchen door. She cupped his chin with her hand and looked into his eyes. "No sense in trying' to reason with a fool", she whispered.

"Now, who wants a piece of still-warm pound cake?" Myra's answer came in the form of squeals of delight from all three children.

That night, Wesley called out to his brother from his bed opposite Nolan's in the large, third-floor bedroom. "Hey, Nolan...what's a homo?"

"I don't know for sure but I think it might be the same as a queer...like old Sammy Carr...you know, the sissy boy that helps his momma at her beauty shop."

"Oh. Well, are you one...a queer, like Pa says?"

"Hell, no!" Nolan tossed a dirty sock across the room at his brother. It missed.

"Sounds like Pa thinks you might be."

"Pa don't know shit. He's just scared that I might be able to do something he can't, the old bastard!"

"Nolan, you better not let Pa hear you talk like that. You know he'll whip your ass for cussin'."

Nolan sat up in bed and switched on the light. "Want to see something I ain't never shown anybody before?"

Wesley nodded. His eyes were wide in anticipation. Nolan was not sure why he was ready to show his little brother his secret. Perhaps, knowing that his teacher believed in his talent had been enough to bolster his resolve. He knew Theo would never approve of art class but it did not matter. Nolan had made up his mind. He wanted to draw and paint and wanted to learn to be the best artist ever. No matter what Theo thought.

Nolan pulled a leftover Christmas box from under his bed. It held drawings of birds and horses, flowers and trees. There were dozens of pictures of varying size, each more life-like than the one before. They were on notebook paper, the back of wrapping paper, envelopes, or anything with a square of white space. Any paper was canvas for Nolan's work.

"Wow, Nolan. Did you draw this?" Wesley had moved to the foot of his brother's bed to survey the artwork. He glanced back and forth at Nolan, as though checking to make sure it was okay to touch the papers. Usually, touching any of Nolan's possession could bring a swift punch.

Nolan slid the box across the bed towards Wesley then watched him, gingerly, pick up each one and hold it to the light. He had drawn most of them entirely in pencil, though some had subtle hues of color, probably from crayons stolen out of Jessie's toy box.

"Can I have one? I mean I won't show it to nobody if you don't want me to." Wesley expected Nolan to kick him off the bed. That would be the norm but, this time, Nolan just nodded and told him to go ahead and pick one out.

Wes wasted no time. "I want this one." He had chosen a picture of a bird in flight with a worm in its beak, soaring towards a nest in a tree. The heads of three baby birds strained up towards her, their mouths open in anticipation, their eyes, realistically, focused towards the mother's approach. The entire drawing was on the back of a slightly crumpled, once

64

discarded envelope with the Rose County Utility Company emblem on the front.

"Why did you pick that one, Wes? It's puny. Here get a better one." Nolan held out the box for his brother to pick again. He knew Wesley was too young to appreciate how much work Nolan had put into that picture. Like its proportion and scale, the attention to detail on the feathers or the way he had used the pencil's eraser to blur, ever so slightly, the wings so it fooled the eye and gave the wings movement. Surely, Nolan thought, his brother would pick one an eight-year-old could appreciate.

"No, I want this one." He was adamant. "I like it best. It looks like the tree outside our window. You know, where the birds build a nest every year and the Mama bird takes care of the babies until they get old enough to fly away. That's why I like it. Plus," Wesley added, "You put your name on this one, kind of like it's autographed." He smiled at Nolan, placed the picture between the mirror and frame of the dresser, and climbed back into bed. "Don't forget now," Wesley sat back up before pulling up the covers, "that one's mine. Don't be an Indian-giver."

With that odd yet endearing expression of brotherly love, along with Mrs. Carson's words of encouragement, Nolan felt a new sense of pride. Perhaps he was destined to be something his father could not. Just maybe, when he grew up he could be something special, maybe a businessman or an artist or, at least, something other than an alcoholic bully.

"Okay, Wes. I promise not to be an Indian-giver."

Deep down, Nolan loved his little brother, but trusted no one. He was especially wary of anyone named Cline, even

Wesley. Before turning out the light, Nolan scoured the room for a new hiding place for his art box.

He could not remember just when he decided to join the Army. Heck, he could not even remember exactly why. However, Nolan did remember that combat was good for one thing- it made you forget the hell you left back home.

After high school, he was determined to get away from Eden Falls and his crazy family. Signing up was as easy as driving thirty miles to Fort Bragg. It had been a hasty decision but one that well-suited Nolan. He had found his calling in the Army and served two, eighteen-month, back-to-back, tours in the Persian Gulf. He was a good at his job. Nolan thought himself as good a soldier as he was an artist and was disappointed when he was denied a third combat tour. He could not imagine the need for a mental health test for possible combat stress. Nolan was so angry with the Army that he chose to opt out of the military, completely.

He figured all war zones were alike, so he might as well fight on domestic soil as foreign. Since the Army forced him out Nolan would just go home and deal with his stress his own way.

That was over four years ago and Nolan still could not deal with his stress. He wished someone understood his pain and, sometimes, he wished he had taken the Army up on some kind of psychological and medical help. However, Nolan knew that would mean being around strangers and having to talk to people. He had never done well with strangers. In fact, outside of his own family, he only had a couple of friends in which he could confide in. On a recent binge-drinking night, he tried to open up to Charlie, his drinking friend, about joining the military.

"It's easy to walk from one world into another, Charlie," Nolan remembered telling him, "You just get up and go. You think you're putting your demons behind you until you walk into third-world combat. Then you live in that hellhole for three years and get introduced to brand new demons that you bring back home with you. Know what I mean, Charlie?" Nolan looked over at his friend and added, "But then, you don't realize that those new demons won't get along good with the old ones, and..."

As the booze hit its mark, it drained all power from Nolan's voice and thought process. No matter. Nolan did not expect his friend to understand. After all, Charlie had not seen the death and misery that war brings. He had not been in the military. In fact, he had never been out of North Carolina. So no, Charlie could never understand, even if he had not passed out ten minutes before.

6.

March 3, 1999
Rachel Kirby

For the third night in a row, Rachel Kirby awoke around two in the morning to discover her husband's side of the bed empty. This confirmed it. Tom's insomnia was worsening. In her haste, she did not attempt to find her slippers in the dark and winced when her bare feet met the shock of cold floorboards. Flickers from the television screen lit a path down the hallway leading to the den and to Tom, who lay slouched and snoring on the couch. He jumped when Rachel touched his shoulder.

"Geez, Rach...don't sneak up on me like that."

"Sorry, but it's late...or early, depending on how you look at the clock. She curled up on his lap and wrapped her arms around him. "This is the third night in a row." Her lips brushed his forehead. "Damn it, Babe. You're starting to worry me."

They had weathered an exhausting holiday season. Coming on the heels of the Jessica Cline murder, this past Christmas had been less festive than usual. Rachel's job had kept her extra busy at the hospital with most of her free time spent helping out with church activities. The season had been tough on them both. Having so little time for each other was enough to put a strain on any marriage, especially one as new as theirs.

Rachel was not worried about their relationship, per say, but she was worried about Tom. Between the two of them, she had always perceived herself emotionally stronger. It seemed she could handle problems easier than he could. He internalized things, allowing trouble to brew and fester while her exorcism of stress and frustration was as easy as spitting out a profanity. Their emotional styles usually counterbalanced perfectly, but not this time. Rachel could see that Tom was becoming preoccupied with Jessica Cline's murder investigation, or, rather the lack thereof.

The murder, which had been daily news for three months, was still unsolved and seemed to be growing cold. Once a front-page headline, the story had crept to the inside pages and, now, to the back of the *News Tribune*. As often happens with such tragedies, it seemed people were already starting to forget. Jessica Cline's name was fading from local conversation and Rachel could see Tom's frustration growing. She knew he felt a need to prevent the case from growing ever colder and she felt powerless to help him.

"I'm sorry, Rach, I know I'm no fun to be around right now but I just can't get her out of my mind." He grabbed his wife and held her close. "No matter a person's lifestyle or how many bad things they've done, no one deserves to die that way, no one should be treated like they are — disposable." He looked into his wife's eyes. "People are not throwaway objects!

"I know you wish I would stop thinking about this case

and — well, maybe you're right. But" — Tom pushed Rachel off his lap and sat up. "She haunts me, and I can't help but think I should try to do something. But, what? I've prayed and prayed without answers. I just don't …"

Rachel interrupted Tom's words with an embrace. Pressing his head onto her shoulder and began to rock back and forth, humming a soothing lullaby. She stroked his hair as though trying to calm a fussy baby and, soon Tom relaxed in her arms and allowed exhaustion to win. Even in sleep, though, Tom was restless, as though his mind could not let go of his thoughts. Rachel suspected Tom was having tortured dreams of the murdered girl he never knew. She had to find a way to help him.

Listening to the phone ring in the parsonage office, Rachel could picture it in her mind. Tom would be five minutes into a much-needed power nap, paralyzed to the couch. He would have just reached the moment of relaxation where he was in a fugue, not quite asleep, vaguely aware of his surroundings but unable to move a muscle. He would decide to let the machine screen the call and the voice would be hers, checking to see that he was okay after what she was certain was a fractious night's sleep in the den. Tom would smile when he heard her say she hoped he was enjoying the power nap she was sure he was taking.

"I know you so well, Tom Kirby." Rachel said before the opening message played through.

Then, when she heard the beep, "I'll be home around four. Oh, by the way, Sweetie, I had an idea this morning. Why don't I give Abby a call tonight when I get home? You know we have wanted her to visit ever since we moved up here. Well, what better time than now? Just a thought—anyway, we will talk about it tonight. See you later. Love you! Bye! — Oh, and enjoy your nap."

Rachel tried to imagine what Tom would do when he heard this message. She knew it would be music to his ears and would fully wake him from his power nap.

Abby was Rachel's best friend and college roommate all four years they attended Emory University. A free spirit and a bit of a daredevil, Abby loved a challenge, especially if it involved solving a mystery. Rachel was angry herself for not thinking of this sooner. Abby was a rookie agent with the FBI's Atlanta office. That could not hurt the situation, either.

7.

March 17, 1999
Abby Rials

S he pulled the little black sports car onto the shoulder of the road and put the car into park. With one hand, Abby pushed the button to release the convertible top while she fumbled through the papers on the passenger seat with the other. She was searching for the North Carolina road map purchased a few miles back where she had stopped for gas and a bite to eat. The map purchase was an afterthought but a wise one it turned out. Since following Rachel's directions to take exit 52, the four lanes of Interstate 95 had morphed into a winding two-lane blacktop with nothing but fields and pastures on the horizon.

Her gas gauge was already flashing yellow so when Abby saw the billboard inviting travelers to "Henry's Gas Station, Seafood Market & Hair Salon", she stopped. Regardless of the unorthodox combination of services, she filled the tank and went inside to pay. That is where she tempted gastronomic fate with a hot dog, nuked in a microwave of the semi-clean establishment and grabbed the North Carolina map.

To Abby's surprise, the hot dog was quite tasty. Still,

she resisted the temptation to go back for another. Good move, she decided, noticing a handwritten sign nailed to a post in front of the store that proudly announced *Get Crabs Here!* Now, that was funny, she thought. As she waited for the canvas top to settle into its carriage behind the seat, Abby made a mental note to share that laugh with Rachel.

She waited to hear the click that signaled the convertible top was safely latched and began cleaning the passenger seat, gathering the paper, notes and napkins that had accumulated during her five-hour trip. Travel trash, as she called it, could be a mess. Abby had already learned the hard way that driving a convertible with the top down could be costly if travel trash became airborne. A well-earned speeding ticket did not bother Abby. She liked to drive fast. However, paying another fifty dollars for a ticket for littering was just plain embarrassing.

Before getting back on the road, Abby scoured the roadmap in search of the city of Eden Falls, North Carolina. Hardly a city, she found it was just a tiny dot on the massive state map, easy to miss without a pair of good reading glasses or fresh contacts and it was just thirty miles away.

Happy to be so close to a reunion with Rachel and Tom, she found herself a bit disappointed that the drive would be a short one. Abby was enjoying the fresh air and beautiful landscape. It was a pleasant change from the urban Atlanta skyline, the inner-city smell, and the monotony of driving the interstate.

Early spring blooms dotted the sides of the highway. Bright green tips of new growth on the evergreens sparkled in the bright morning sun. She slowed to admire the view and noticed a farmer on his tractor, preparing his field for planting. He threw up his hand in a friendly wave as she drove by. How nice, she thought. The bucolic scene was refreshing and she caught herself feeling a bit jealous of Rachel being in this peaceful place all the time.

Wait a minute. That thought brought Abby back to reality. All the time? Not for her but it did seem like the perfect environment to tame her party-loving, foul-mouthed, best friend. Yes, Rachel would need the perfect environment and the perfect man to change her bad habits. Thank God, she had Tom Kirby.

Poor Tom, she thought. Abby often felt sorry for him. The challenge of calming Rachel would be a monumental job but, if anyone could do it, Tom Kirby could. He was kind to a fault. He would do anything for Rachel and she for him. Abby hoped to find a love like that one day.

For now, Abby's only love was her job. Although still considered a rookie, she loved the excitement of being an FBI agent in one of the most crime-riddled cities in the country. There was so much to learn and the fast-paced environment left little time for a social life. For months, Abby had worked nonstop so she was looking forward to a quiet weekend just catching up with her friends. It would be great to kick back and put bad people out of her mind for a couple of days.

Abby recalled Rachel's phone call from last week. She mentioned a local murder case that she might want some input on from Abby; said it was unsolvable. After nearly a year with the Bureau, the one thing she was sure of was that no case is unsolvable. Abby was certain the state and local law enforcement had a handle on the case by now. After all, that was months ago.

Following the map and Rachel's instructions Abby found the turn to Bethel Church in less than fifteen minutes. She even saw the church steeple in the distance. Rounding a curve, the white clapboard church and its bell tower came into view, its green patina of the past hundred years covering its copper top, just as Rachel had described. The churchyard and adjoining cemetery were well manicured and set an appropriate distance from the sanctuary. She caught a whiff of fresh-mowed grass, its geometric designs from the mower blades still glistened in the morning sun. It was quaint and looked like a postcard.

Abby was still taking in the beauty of the landscape when she saw Rachel standing on the steps of the house next door, grinning and waving. As she turned into the drive, her friend was jumping up and down with excitement. This was going to be fun.

The two spent the afternoon sitting at the kitchen table, sipping Cokes and catching up on the past year apart. They gossiped and giggled as always.

"Where's Tom?" Abby had asked.

"He's in his study putting the finishing touches on Sunday's sermon. Tom!" Rachel called back down the hallway.

"Tom! He probably can't hear me. He gets all into his work by the end of the week. He'll join us soon, I'm sure."

Abby sensed a little tension in her friend's voice with that last statement.

Tom was pleased to see his wife so happy. Abby's visit would be a nice respite from the stressful past few months. It might be good for him, too. Maybe it would get his mind off the dismal winter. Seeing a familiar face might even help his own moodiness.

Whom was he kidding? Tom knew he was lying to himself. Sure, he was happy for Rachel to see her old friend but, truth was, Abby's FBI connection was all he could think about since she had confirmed her visit. Even before greeting his wife's best friend, he wondered how soon he could breach the subject of her helping with the case.

He wondered how much Rachel had told her on the phone. What did she know about the murder? Had Rachel told her anything about Jessica Cline? Was she aware of how important her help might be? Tom wanted to run into the kitchen, interrupt them and ask Abby these questions. Instead, he tried to calm himself down and wait for the right time.

"Don't let me interrupt. Just want to say hello." He hugged Abby and added, "Great to see you, Abby. Sorry, but I was just finishing my sermon for Sunday. We'll catch up later — promise." Tom walked back down the hall and closed his office door behind him.

He tried to sound normal and not show his nervousness. After obsessing for days about asking Abby for help in solving Jessica Cline's murder, suddenly he was finding it difficult to ask for such a favor.

Tom returned to his desk and tried to concentrate. He

shuffled papers, refilled his stapler, and even wrote himself a reminder to pick up his clothes from the dry cleaners and stuck it on the edge of his lampshade to emphasize its importance. Nothing, it seemed was helping him keep his mind off the obvious.

He turned his chair around and stared out the window, trying not to listen to the happy chatter coming from the kitchen. The sounds made him smile. Their animated voices almost drowned out that other voice he had begun to hear, a voice that was getting louder and stronger every day. Soon, he feared the only one he would be able to hear would be one from the grave.

His office window provided a stunning view of Bethel's side lawn. Bright blue-green tips of the cedars and tiny white cones on the pine trees gave the first hint of new growth. Tendrils hanging from the Bradford pears that lined the parking lot were full of buds about to burst into full bloom. This promise of a new season was nature's own message of hope. That, alone, should be enough inspiration for any preacher to write a wonderful sermon.

Tom was about to do just that when his eyes were drawn to that quiet place behind the fellowship hall, the place that commanded more of his attention than it should. As he stared at Jessica Cline's gravesite, he succumbed to the voice that now followed him everywhere.

"Please don't forget me." She pleaded.

"I know you think we are taking advantage of your friendship, Abby, but we thought..." Tom corrected himself and continued. "I was wondering if there was anything you can do to help us. I mean, with your knowledge and FBI connections…"

Tom was sure Rachel had told her pretty much everything by now but he had no idea what she was thinking. "I know you're busy and may not have much time to do anything but…" Tom realized he had turned into a blubbering, stammering fool who was begging his wife's best friend for help. How pathetic he thought.

"Whoa, now hold on a minute. I hope you don't think there's much I can do about a local case on the FBI level." Abby had already shared with Rachel that she did not think she could be of any help on this case.

Tom looked disappointed. He had hoped Abby would be willing to review the details of the case.

"Okay, listen – you know I've never shied away from this kind of challenge," Abby paused then reached out, grabbing her friends by the hand. "I'm only here for two days."

The crestfallen look on Rachel's face made Abby quickly add, "So let's get going!"

With those words, Tom provided a two-hour dissertation on the life and death of Jessica Cline.

In spite of her reluctantly accepted challenge, the remainder of the weekend visit was great fun. Abby and Rachel stayed up late catching up on all the news of their personal lives. So much had changed for both of them during the past year. It was hard to believe that they were grown up, adults with real jobs and responsibilities. College and graduation seemed like a lifetime ago instead of the mere eighteen months it had actually been.

Saturday morning, Rachel took Abby on a tour of Eden Falls where she saw the slower lifestyle of Rose County. She introduced Abby to as many friends and acquaintances as possible, each one friendly and welcoming. By that afternoon, Abby saw why Rachel and Tom had been smitten with this community. Indeed, it seemed like the perfect little town.

Sunday morning, Abby sat on the front row of Bethel Baptist Church, listening to Tom's sermon about God's promise of a new season. She managed to glance around the room, recognizing many of the faces as those she had met the day before. Tom gave the prayer of benediction while her eyes, irreverently, scanned the congregation, all heads bowed in prayer. Those who filled the church pews that day looked to be the epitome of good Christians who, no doubt, led clean, near-perfect lives. Surely, none of them would ever commit an illegal or immoral act.

Abby had to force herself not to snicker aloud. This group of folks with their heads bowed looked so absurdly pious but Abby knew better. These people were no different here than any other small town – or big city, for that matter.

She looked over at Rachel, surprised to see her friend take on the same angelic appearance as the others in the congregation. Same bowed head, eyes closed in rapt devotion. Abby wondered if the fine folks of Eden Falls had discovered yet that the sweet preacher's wife cussed like a sailor and could, on occasion, drink like one, too? After living here this long, Rachel must have let more than one vulgarity slip.

If so, neither Rachel nor the "flock" let that nugget show. Most likely, everyone knew but, politely, hid it. Could someone here hide other dirty, little secrets? Suddenly Abby was more confident that her decision to look into Jessica Cline's murder was the right one.

As the praying ended, Abby found her mind wandering and her questions growing. Did folks think this case unsolvable? That it would be too hard to bring anyone to justice. Did they think the killer was far away and no longer a threat to residents of this community? Were they okay with thinking a killer had moved on, now a problem for some other small town? Maybe they assumed another community had a poor soul to sacrifice, their own version of a drug-addicted prostitute to spare. Abby suddenly felt like she had entered the plot of "The Stepford Wives". Had the whole community been brainwashed? Did no one care or was someone hiding the truth?

After a delicious Sunday dinner at the parsonage, the three washed and dried the dishes while enjoying small talk. Abby's compliments to Tom on his sermon and Rachel on the great meal were sincere, unlike the vibe she got from the residents of Eden Falls.

She did not voice her concerns to Tom and Rachel choosing, instead, to save judgment for another trip back to North Carolina.

"I'll get back home and gather some equipment and supplies from the office. I have a couple of weeks of vacation coming. What better place to spend it than right here with my best friends?"

Abby found herself getting excited at the prospect of

returning to the area. It had been great to see Rachel again and this visit had been too short. She would love to explore more of this lovely place. Besides, she was intrigued at what secrets lay buried in this perfect little Garden Of Eden Falls.

8.

April 9, 1999
Tom Kirby

Still No Leads in Halloween Murder. Tom read the headline, buried on page four of *The News Tribune* and accompanied by two forgettable paragraphs. Apparently, a story that was once the crime of the century had become back page news for every paper in the state. Tom was not sure at what point the life and death of Jessica Cline became insignificant but it had happened in less than six months. Now, the story was little more than filler for media outlets, a convenient insert between slick advertisements for antihistamine sales at Revco and coupons touting dollar-off bunny shaped Easter cakes at Piggly Wiggly.

Tom slid the newspaper across the desk hard enough to sail it into the trashcan at the opposite end. He knew the *Tribune* had tried to keep the story alive but, with no headway towards solving the case, there was simply nothing to print. Local and state authorities claimed to have thoroughly investigated the evidence. Their conclusions were unanimous.

"Jessica Cline was picked up by an unknown person as she walked down Highway 37 on the morning of October 31, 1998." Sheriff Omar Sanders said during the most recent press conference on the killing. "It appears the motive was rape and/or robbery. Perhaps the victim resisted or maybe even tried to rob her assailant." The article went on to state that, while no one could be certain of what happened, it was clear that the victim may have, in part, contributed to the assault. In other words, regardless of the details, Jessica Cline wound up the loser in a dangerous game she had played, successfully, may times in the past.

The *Tribune* had stopped short of stating in print that Jessica had it coming to her. The inference was that of blaming the victim. Since no new clues to the killer had been uncovered, officials had tagged the case, unofficially, "cold".

Tom walked around his desk and retrieved the crumpled paper from the trash basket. He smoothed out as many creases as possible before doing what he had done with every single bit of information he had gathered about the murder. He placed it in the box he was saving for Abby's return.

Banker's boxes and cardboard cartons were stacked on the basement floor of Bethel Baptist Church. They contained file folders, copies of handwritten notes, and newspaper clippings. When those were full, laundry baskets and grocery bags held every scrap of paper Tom had found having anything to do with the case.

Rachel had dubbed the seldom-used lower-level area below the sanctuary the "war room", a harsh if not downright sacrilegious tag. Tom felt uneasy about it until he thought about the fact that local law enforcement did not seem able to solve the crime. After deciding this would be the best use of the space and after praying about it, Tom simply asked God to bless the events that would take place there and watch over them as they worked.

Abby had been in close contact with Tom and Rachel since her visit and agreed that the unused church basement would be the safest place to work on the investigation. After her returned to Atlanta, she had called often, making sure Tom and Rachel set up the war room by her specifications. She had shipped several items the previous week and now, a laptop computer, printer, and briefcase were among the investigative items locked safely inside the labyrinth of the church. If Tom and Rachel wanted to solve this case, it would have to be a certain way—Abby's way. She had made that clear in her daily calls to them.

Her instructions on the war room's setup had been precise, as well. Tom tried to follow and expand on those directions. Old chalkboards and corkboards no longer used for Sunday school classes were handy for practical, low-tech use. Along the walls, Tom had placed worktables to hold the high-speed internet equipment, which was impressive state-of-the-art technology for 1998. After a little research, Tom found they could run internet cable off the second, seldom-used, telephone line. Abby would have access to the FBI's latest investigative tools with the input of her government identification and passwords. Tom would make sure to reimburse the church, discretely of course, for any expenses. Ever honest with church coffers, he would never take a penny from his parishioners even if he thought it would help bring a killer to justice.

It had taken Tom most of two days to set up the war room in preparation for Abby's return. The large wall clock, a recent purchase, caught his attention. He had to finish by six o'clock when the Men's Baptist Union met upstairs in the sanctuary. Tom would not want members to show up early and come looking for him down here. No need to raise suspicion even before the activities start.

The last item Tom brought down to the basement was a crosscut shredder, bought at Office Mart the day before. The shredder had been one of Abby's specific needs, that, and chalk, plenty of chalk.

It was five-thirty when Tom turned out the lights and prepared to lock the door. The war room was ready for battle. Feeling like he had forgotten something, he opened the door again and flipped the light back on. Tom fumbled through one of the boxes until he found a fat new piece of chalk and walked over to the chalkboard in the center of the room. Just under the colorful alphabet frame of the board that once held Bible verses for kindergarteners, Tom wrote in large block print — **WHO KILLED JESSICA CLINE?**

Once again, the little black BMW drove up the now familiar parsonage driveway and parked in the back alongside Rachel's car. It had been two weeks since Abby's return to Atlanta to finalize her request for two weeks' vacation time. After a year of working extra hours and not taking any sick days, she had earned nearly a month of vacation time, and she was ready for the time off.

"Honey, I'm home!" Abby joked as Rachel ran out to greet her. They hugged.

"Boy, I'm glad to see you!" Rachel reached into the backseat to help with Abby's bags. "Just wait until you see the conference room Tom has set up for us. After you rest a bit, I will show it to you. It really turned out great!" Unable to contain her excitement, she was talking ninety miles per hour as she placed Abby's bags in the guest room.

"At least give the girl a cup of coffee." Tom was standing in the hallway shaking his head. "Hi, Abby. Welcome back." He, too, greeted her with a big hug.

"I'm really not that tired. I stopped four times on the way up. Why don't you give me a minute to change clothes and give me the tour?" Abby found herself excited, as well.

The three surveyed the workspace, as Rachel pointed out each area with the enthusiasm of a cruise ship director showing off ice sculptures at the midnight buffet.

"So, what do you think? Isn't it perfect?" Rachel was, obviously, proud of her husband's work.

"I must say. This really is impressive." Abby replied.

After being reassured of the security of the location, they agreed to begin work later that evening. "But, first," Abby stated, "I need to unpack and share a most wonderful gastronomic find with you two." Abby had stopped at Henry's, the same gas station, grill, and bait store she found on her first visit. This time, she had not only purchased her hot dogs "to go", she had brought Rachel & Tom lunch as well.

"Okay, guys. All we have to do is microwave these for 30 seconds." She held the paper bag in front of her friends who were speechless. "I learned that the brand is *Bright Leaf* hot dogs and they are only sold in this part of North Carolina. And they're delish!"

She could tell Tom and Rachel were skeptics and probably thought Abby was a little crazy but she was happy to show them something new about their adopted home state. She would explain the ominous bait shop origin later, knowing they would find it funny. She was really trying to start this visit off by lightening the mood.

"Now, let's nuke these suckers!"

Abby was right, all agreed. *Bright Leaf* hotdogs were a wonderful find.

Later that evening, the three pulled up chairs facing each other inside the large, locked basement. Tom and Rachel looked to Abby to begin.

Having witnessed their enthusiasm for causes in years past, Abby feared it was entirely possible that her friends' expectations may not be realistic. She decided to begin with a disclaimer, one she had rehearsed on the drive up Interstate 20 from Atlanta.

"Okay, guys, before anyone gets their hopes fixed on sending a killer to prison for life, I just want to warn you," Abby paused and pulled her chair up close, "that may never happen. It's just a fact."

Abby continued. "We may not be able to solve this crime and I don't want to set you up for a big disappointment." She made note of the disbelieving expression on Tom's face and added, "I promise to do everything I can to help you but, remember, I only have two weeks before I have to get back to work and you two are on your own… just want to be realistic here."

Tom stood up, assuming his "preacher" persona.

"Abby, we're not stupid. We don't expect the impossible but we do know how good you are at your job. We really appreciate you giving up vacation time to be here. We will simply do whatever we can with the time we have and, if we are not successful, well… at least we tried. At least we didn't do - nothing."

"Okay then." Abby jumped up and grabbed the banker's box nearest her. "The clock's ticking! Let's get started."

She picked up the nearly new piece of chalk from the table and, taking care not to disturb Tom's boldly under-lined question, wrote CRIME SCENE underneath it. As she pulled the first files from the box, she began to list each fact on the board. Abby gestured for Rachel and Tom to do the same.

For three hours, they picked out and listed every fact about the crime scene. After combining repetitive details, the three sleuths listed each new fact until all the data was facing them on five separate chalkboards.

"Wow, this looks like a whole lot of…." Tom searched for a word.

"Shit." Rachel chimed in. "What can shit tell us?"

"No it's a beginning." Abby reminded them that these were clues. "You guys have been watching too much television. What, right now, looks like scattered pieces of a jigsaw puzzle will soon become a picture, maybe a picture of a kill-er? We just have to examine each piece and put this puzzle together. Now, let's get some rest – sounds like Rachel really needs it, and we can begin again tomorrow."

As Tom turned out the lights and stood looking from the door into the war room. The girls were waiting at the top of the stairs.

"Tom?" Rachel called out to him.

Tom bounded up the stairs. "Sorry. I was just thinking."

"About what?" Rachel was ready to get to bed.

"Just thinking how much I hate jigsaw puzzles." Tom answered.

The following morning, Abby had the war room to herself. Rachel still had two more days to work at the hospital before she could take time off and Tom would be handling church business as usual. Abby relished the time to organize the workspace and catch up with the details of the case. While she had studied the case before she got here, the ability to review the details closer to the crime scene were more than helpful.

She turned on the radio mainly to drown out the "quiet" of being alone in a church basement on a Monday morning. Rachel had been sweet to remember how much Abby loved music. Still, she had warned, there were only two local stations and only one that carried more than the weather forecast and farm report. Abby was happy to learn that WOKZ was, indeed, a music station. She started the day's work with Martha and the Vandellas singing in the background. She had quickly learned that WOKZ was an oldies station, which suited Abby just fine.

She pulled up an empty chalkboard on which she memorialized with details about the victim. Soon, facts surrounding the last ten years of Jessica Cline's life appeared. Rachel had uncovered medical reports documenting Jessica's illnesses and injuries going back to 1984. A laundry list of problems, not just medical, but social and legal began to come into focus, the dates and times often connecting or, sometimes, overlapping. This made an interesting way to cross-reference information.

Abby was able to use a time-tested FBI method of assimilating facts and applying a specific formula to identify patterns of behavior. She had seen it done at the Bureau but had never really used it on her own. Here was her chance to see how much she had learned from her mentors.

Abby saw that over a four-year period, Jessica Cline was a frequent complainant or detainee on a police report. Between 1984 and 1988, she was involved in public drunkenness, fighting, disturbing the peace, driving while impaired, or no operator's license. From 1989 until 1991, the charges included marijuana and/or drug paraphernalia. When she placed Jessica's rap sheet alongside her medical records, they nearly paralleled.

Legal records showed that family members were, at first, willing to get her out of jail. They even hired a lawyer for her, on occasion. Eventually, she was back in jail, spending days, sometimes weeks, locked up because her mother would not or possibly could not, put up her bond or hire an attorney. It appeared her family had grown tired of giving her second and third chances. Abby noted three judicial recommendations that Jessica seek alcohol and drug rehabilitation. Since there was no documented treatment or follow-up to this order, Jessica must have received none.

Abby poured another cup of coffee while she waited for requested follow-up information on any possible out-of-state treatment for Jessica's drug and alcohol use. It would not take long to check the records so Abby waited beside the fax machine in anticipation. Before long, the fax machine began to sputter out pages, none of which showed treatment facilities that may have admitted Jessica Cline.

The rhythmic tap of the fax machine had printed out six pages when Abby heard a vehicle driving up outside. She pulled up a chair and, standing on tiptoes, peered through the small egress window near the ceiling. All she could see was the tires and rear of a vehicle but the silver license plate marked *Permanent*, was her giveaway. It was a patrol car. Abby froze and watched a deputy step from the driver's side. A spit-polished shine on the shoes matched the razor-sharp crease on the gray pants but that was all she could see of the officer. She pictured Barney Fife.

She listened as the sound of slow, steady footsteps crunched the gravel as he walked across the drive and wondered if he could hear the music from the radio in the basement, or the sound of the fax machine still spitting out paper. Unable to reach the printer from her perch, Abby was ready to reach over and pull the plug from the wall when she heard Tom's voice outside.

"Hey, James, how's it going?" Apparently, Tom knew the officer. Abby breathed a sigh of relief when she heard the footsteps walking away. The fax continued to push out pages at a steady click.

"Just out this way on patrol, Reverend Kirby. Thought I would walk through and make sure everything's okay out here. You know they had some church break-ins over in Duplin County last week. They got away. So, we want to keep our eyes open around here."

The voices were getting faint. Thank goodness, Abby thought. Tom is leading him away from the open basement windows.

"Sure do appreciate that, James. It would be a shame to

lose anything out here. I usually notice when someone drives up but I will pay particular attention now that I know a burglar may be on the prowl.

The footsteps abruptly stopped.

"Wow, Preacher! Looks like you got yourself a new car!" The deputy had spotted Abby's convertible.

"Oh, no" Tom chuckled. "That's not mine. It belongs to a friend who's visiting for a few days." Tom was trying to steer James Wilcox towards the house and away from the church.

"Man that's a sweet ride. Your friend has good taste! I would love to have something like that one day. He must make a bundle – your friend, I mean. What does he do?" Wilcox eyed the BMW with envy.

"Actually, it's a *she*, Rachel's college roommate, that is. She works for — ah — she's a book editor in Atlanta. Maybe you will be able to meet her sometime. She and Rachel are not here right now- gone to town. Anyway, thanks for stopping by."

Tom had managed to get Wilcox back to his patrol car. "It's good to know you're keeping an eye out for us, James. Well, guess I had better get back to writing this week's sermon.

"Sure thing, Tom. Here is my business card, in case you see anything unusual or need me. It has my home and business numbers. You know I grew up in this church. Sure don't want to have anything happen to it on my watch." Just before getting back in the car, he turned is head toward the basement window. "What's that noise?"

Tom turned towards the window, as well. He was trying

to think of something to say when, as if by magic, the fax machine stopped its rhythmic sputter.

"I don't hear anything." Tom breathed a sigh of relief that he would not have to repent for telling more than two lies in the same conversation.

"I don't hear it now, either. Oh well, must be hearing things." James shook his head as he climbed into his cruiser and rolled the window down. He reminded Tom to call if he needed help.

Waving until James was out of sight, Tom went straight to the basement. He was sure Abby must be concerned.

"That was close," she said. "What did Barney Fife want?" She did not seem worried but added, "He nearly made me pull the plug on this data from the Bureau, but it came through just fine." She began to read the first page as Tom answered her question.

"That was Deputy James Wilcox." Tom began, adding his reasons for stopping by and his relationship to the church but Abby was barely listening. Mesmerized by the faxed report, multiple pages of out-of-state police records. It seemed Jessica Cline was, indeed, in the FBI system and had a rap sheet that crisscrossed the country.

Tom was talking about what a nice guy James Wilcox was when Abby interrupted him.

"Oh, now this is interesting! Did you know about this?"

Abby twirled around and shoved the paper at Tom. It was a birth certificate and attached adoption papers.

Tom looked so shocked to see the information that he completely missed his telephone ringing on the main line.

"Tom. Answer the phone." Abby realized the fax had

taken him by surprise. "I can't answer that line." She grabbed the paper from his hands, shoving him towards the ringing phone. She could tell that church business would interrupt things for now.

"You, go back to work. We will meet here tonight. Maybe I'll have more information by then."

She watched Tom walk back to the house, shaking his head in obvious frustration. As she began to reorganize the war room to make the space more efficient, more like an official Bureau war room, she felt renewed motivation and confidence, along with a hint of smugness. Abby was thrilled at how quickly she was able to obtain this new information.

It was nearly seven when Tom unlocked the church basement and turned on the lights. Abby watched the faces of her friends as they saw the new and improved war room for the first time. *Underwhelmed,* Abby thought.

"Looks nice, Abby," Rachel said. "I'll put on a pot of coffee."

Abby smiled, realizing her friends did not understand that there was an art to the order of details when investigating a crime. Rachel and Tom had no frame of reference to the process drilled into Abby at the Academy.

Like the teacher beginning a lesson, Abby began with the first chalkboard, pointing to and reading, aloud, each offense, which seemed to repeat so often it started to get boring. Moving to the next chalkboard, the facts took on a more sinister tone.

"This seems to be where her life turns a little darker." Abby glanced over to make sure her friends were paying attention. They were.

"In July 1990, Jessica called 911 to report being beaten by her brother, although she did not identify which one. When deputies arrived, she recanted, refusing to identify which brother she had accused. It was clear she was, once again, drunk. After interviewing the Clines, the deputies hauled Jessica to jail. The charge?-Falsely accusing Nolan, or Wesley, of assault."

"Then, one week later," Abby paused to take a sip of coffee. "Jessica called for help again, saying her brothers *and* her father had assaulted her. This time, the bruises on her face made the deputies question the Cline men a little more closely. Interrogated separately, they told the same story; she was intoxicated; she fell down the steps.

Abby passed the faxed report to Tom and motioned for them to look it over. She sat on the conference table, swinging her legs as though she were on a playground, and waited. She desperately wanted her friends to find the clue hidden on the page.

"Well?" Abby asked.

"Well, what? Isn't this the exact same thing you have on the board?" Tom sounded irritated.

"Ah, not exactly", she jumped off the table and back into teacher mode. "Look at it again." Abby wanted to teach her friends how to look at evidence with investigative eyes.

"Look at the paper. Do you notice anything different on this report? Anything in pen?"

Rachel squinted as she took a closer look. She pointed to something in the margins.

"Yeah, looks like a squiggle. No, it's a question mark, a tiny, handwritten, question mark." She looked back at Abby.

"So?"

Abby could tell Rachel and Tom were still underwhelmed.

"I know that both of you have seen some of these reports before I got here, but you saw the transcribed version, not the original, on scene, report. That little scribbled question mark tells me that someone, probably the deputy who wrote it, may have doubted the Cline's story."

"Damn, I'm impressed!" Rachel said.

"Lesson over," Abby squeezed Rachel's hand and added, "Almost."

Paying close attention, Tom and Rachel watched and listened as Abby continued to read from the chalkboard.

"Jessica left town the next day without telling anyone. She was gone for nearly a year." Abby dusted chalk from her hands and added. "That tiny question mark may change my opinion of her reasons for leaving town. How 'bout you?"

Her friends nodded in agreement and Abby felt she, indeed, had made her case for obtaining original documents whenever possible. She realized, too, that the three of them might be able to help solve this case or, at least, warm it up from a cold case.

"Now, the lesson's over." Abby laughed. "It's time for a break."

When their work resumed, they started the next report. Sometime before August19, 1991 Jessie was back in Eden Falls as evidenced by her arrest on that date. This time, though, she asked to see a mental health worker. While the report made no mention of the type care she received, Jessie's name did not appear on the records for

96

several months.

Her next arrest, in 1992, included charges for drug use and prostitution, proving that whatever happened during her implied mental health treatment had only hardened her criminal activity. When Abby read the list of identical charges that followed in rapid succession, it was clear that Jessie's pattern was set.

For about a year, Jessie stayed in the area, drifting between her parents' home and that of her boyfriend, Ashton but she never stayed near home for too long. It seemed she had a talent, second only to that of turning tricks. She was good at disappearing at will, a craft at which she became prolific during the last six years of her life.

Abby stepped back to review the chalkboards and said, "So, here's what we've got so far. What do you see?"

"A sad, sad, life…" Rachel's voice trailed off.

Without taking his eyes off the words on the chalkboards, Tom asked, "What about the information you got earlier? I don't see it here."

"I have that little nugget of information over there." Abby pointed to the covered board standing in the corner. With the flair of a magician pulling a rabbit from a hat, Abby whisked off the cover to reveal a corkboard. Its title, made up of colorful kindergarten stencils, pinned to the top that read: NEW CLUES. The first clue listed underneath was, "birth certificate".

"Have either of you heard anyone say that Jessie had a baby?"

Tom and Rachel replied in tandem, "No!"

Abby slapped her hands together and jumped from her

seat. "And this is how we will find Jessie's murderer – investigating new clues, starting with this one."

A sudden wave of fatigue washed over Abby. It had been a long, but satisfying day.

9

May 2, 1999

Abby Rials

The Sunday morning worship service at Bethel Baptist Church was just like the others Abby had attended with one exception. This day's congregation included Deputy James Wilcox who had accompanied his mother to church that morning.

"Great sermon, Preacher." Abby heard the familiar voice as she exited the sanctuary and a picture of Barney Fife flashed through her memory.

"Ms. Wilcox, I'd like to introduce you to Abby Rials, Rachel's friend from college. Abby, Mrs. Wilcox and her son live over on Highland Road. They are lifelong members of the church. James is a deputy sheriff - in fact he was out here just the other day – looking out for our safety." Tom gave Abby a little nod.

Abby acknowledged Tom's subtlety with a polite handshake and a, "So nice to meet you Mrs. Wilcox."

As she turned to greet the deputy, Abby expected to see a caricature of Mayberry's finest; one that matched the shiny boots she had seen out the basement window. Instead, Abby found herself staring into the beautiful blue eyes of

James Wilcox. Tall and tan, he was quite a contrast to the tiny elderly woman he helped down the church steps. His boyish grin framed perfect snow-white teeth and his sun-streaked blonde hair matched his rugged good looks. He walked with an air of confidence, as though he was proud of escorting his mom to church and, for Abby, something about that seemed so nice. One thing was certain; James Wilcox was no Barney Fife.

Tom broke what was becoming an awkward silence. "James, meet Abby." The two shook hands and exchanged pleasantries.

Sunday dinner was a full spread at the parsonage. Abby was accustomed to eating meals alone, often at her desk at work so a three-course meal in the middle of the day was a treat. As they ate, Tom teased Abby about meeting the most eligible bachelor in Rose County.

Abby tried to ignore him. "I'll do the dishes, Rachel – you cooked such a wonderful meal. Go rest up before we get back into the war room."

"Let's go over the list of persons of interest again before we try to figure out who fathered Jessica's baby." Abby began the Sunday night investigative session. "That may have a lot of impact on the case." The others nodded in agreement.

She walked over to the list of names written on a separate board & flipped the first page to reveal the names that now had a picture beside each one.

"We've been over these folks, seems like a million times." Abby turned to her friends. "But let's review the possible suspects once more." She caught a glimpse of Rachel's eye-roll to Tom.

"Just once more" Abby insisted.

"First, the most obvious: ASHTON CONNORS."

A picture of Jessica's boyfriend stared down at them from his most recent mug shot. Bulging, glassy eyes were the only parts of his face that were not covered with either dirt or hair. Ashton's hair hung in matted clumps that more resembled a neglected poodle than purposely-braided dreadlocks. Looking more like the son of a cave dweller, one would never suspect his father was North Carolina State Senator, William Connors, Jr.

According to records, no one was sure what had caused the Senator's younger son to take a path of self-destruction but Ashton had chosen alcohol and drugs over the family legacy. Older brother, William, III -"Trey" to his friends, was a local physician with a flourishing practice. Clearly, Trey was more like the senator.

Following his wife's death, Senator Connors' attempts to manage Ashton, then a twenty-year-old man-child, failed miserably.

"Truth is," Abby held up a document and summarized, "to the public, Connors disowned his youngest son while becoming his enabler in private. A little house just outside of town proved a convenient place for Ashton to live; a place he could drink and get high without complaining neighbors. As long as the senator paid Ashton's expenses and Trey managed his brother's medical care, both Ashton and the senator's political career appeared solvent. And it was a setup that worked well – most of the time."

"I heard a good story about those two – Ashton and

Jessie – from James Wilcox." Tom chimed in.

"Let's hear it." Abby said.

"He said they were well known around town as a flamboyant couple who did not mind displaying public affection or abuse, sometimes both in the same afternoon. As drinking and drug buddies who met in grade school, most folks knew their love ran hot and cold. They were in a relationship, albeit nothing serious, for the last five years of her life. When she was around Rose County, not off on one of her "world travels", she spent as much time at Ashton's house as with her parents. The Jessica and Ashton often walked along Highway 37, headed towards the nearest convenience store in Eden Falls. Sometimes, they walked the creek bank, a shortcut to bootlegger, Pop Melvin's hideaway in the swamp, before walking home, weaving, wobbling, and laughing, happy as clams, all the way.

Abby sat a little straighter in her chair as she listened to Tom's story.

"Did you say James Wilcox told you this?" Abby tapped her fingernails on the table and stared a half smile to Rachel.

"Oh my God! I know what you're thinking!" Rachel laughed, then high-fived Abby. It was as though she had read her friend's mind.

"Tom, can you get me a date with that cute Deputy Wilcox? Time for a little undercover work."

Abby and Rachel giggled like schoolchildren. Tom just shook his head.

Whose idea was this, anyway?

"Oh yes, I think it was mine." Abby realized she was talking to herself, aloud but why she would ever volunteer to do such a thing. Being around her childhood friend made Abby revert to adolescence and offer to go on a date with James Wilcox just to try to get information about Jessica Cline's murder. Oh, well. Everything is fair in love and war. "And this is war."

Stepping back to review herself in the full-length mirror, Abby realized it was the first time in ages that she was actually concerned about her looks. Just slipping her long dark ponytail from its utilitarian elastic band felt odd and, now, she was unsure about her outfit. Aside from a Sunday dress, she picked very few feminine clothes. Jeans and tees had seemed the more appropriate for her return to Eden Falls. She was glad she thought to toss in the outfit she now wore. The short black skirt showed off her size two figure and the Carolina blue sweater, cleverly added in hopes of gaining brownie points from the locals, accented her deep sapphire eyes. The outfit had been one of those last minute additions to her bag, thrown in just in case she went with Rachel and Tom to Raleigh, Charlotte, or somewhere fun.

She had no idea where James was taking her, so she had no idea if her outfit was even appropriate to wear. She was certain, though, that Rose County had nothing like the infamous Underground Atlanta so she hoped her sweater did not show too much cleavage for wherever it was they were going. Was her skirt too short? She wanted to look neither sexy nor prudish. She was obsessing but could not help herself and after taking a long second look, Abby smiled back at the mirror's reflection.

"Damn, I look good!"

It was her first date in months and that was, probably, why

she was a little nervous. On the other hand, was it because the gorgeous James Wilcox astounded her with his smile? Perhaps it was a little of both. She had to remind herself that this date was not for fun but to gain information. Never one to worry about bending the truth to get facts from a suspect, Abby knew this situation was different. James was different. She considered canceling the date as a completely silly idea but, before she had time to fret further, Rachel came in to tell her James was waiting downstairs.

"Damn, Girl. You look great!"

"That's just what I was saying to myself." Abby beamed.

"Now, remember, I'm not sure if our little James has ever been on a real date, so be gentle with him." Rachel teased. They both giggled and reverted to girlfriend mode with all the excitement of sappy, prom night expectations.

Rachel prattled on, "...and don't mention Jessica Cline...or the murder...unless he brings it up. But, then, why would he..."

"Rachel, will you shut up? You sound like my mama! I know what I'm doing. This is my field of expertise, remember?" Abby realized she had to go through with the date. "All fair in love and murder investigations."

Rachel did not act offended at being cut off by Abby and, giving a nod of approval, whisked Abby out the door to greet James.

Engrossed in sports talk with Tom, James turned to Abby and flashed that beautiful smile. When he turned to greet her, his eyes held a sparkle that Abby took as subliminally meant for her alone and, for just a second, Abby thought she saw it. Could James Wilcox be a "twofer"?

Growing up, Abby and Rachel were like sisters who shared hopes, dreams and secrets. They had made up the code word, "twofer", early on when they decided that they could only be happy in life if they found their one true love, their soul mate. They would never settle for less than perfect and they would make sure, as best friends, both found that true love each deserved. He must be perfect in every way, both handsome and smart. Finding that perfect mate, one with looks and brains, would make him a "twofer". Soon after starting college, Rachel found her "twofer" in Tom Kirby yet in the five years since, Abby had met no one who came close to being as perfect as Tom. The chances of stumbling onto another "twofer" in close proximity to her friend's husband seemed impossible.

"About as impossible as finding Jessica Cline's murderer", Abby mumbled aloud as she walked into the room. She had not meant to say that aloud.

James turned to greet Abby. "Wow. You look lovely tonight."

He seemed temporarily speechless at her appearance but made a quick recovery.

"Were you asking me something? I'm sorry. Tom and I were caught up in the game and I didn't catch what you said."

"No, nothing," Abby smiled up at James and placed her hand in his.

"I hope an informal dinner before the movie is okay." James said as he held open the car door. "You have to understand, fine dining doesn't really exist in Eden Falls."

Anywhere is fine with me." Abby already felt more comfortable around him than most other first dates.

The evening consisted of dinner at Geno's Pizza Palace and the nine o'clock showing of *Titanic*. She found James charming, comfortable to be around and easy to talk to. The conversation soon turned to books, a not so surprising subject given Tom's lie to James about Abby's profession. She made a mental note to get her revenge at Tom for that one but, for now, the task was how to carry on an intelligent conversation about books.

She had heard James, clearly, ask about her favorite authors but she stalled. "Let's see. My favorite author, you ask. Or did you ask about my favorite book? – It's just that I have so many manuscripts to read, I have very little time to read for pleasure.

"Let's see...I like Pat Conroy, for one. What about you?" In true investigative style, she deflected the question back to James. His answer surprised her.

"Oh, nothing compares to the old guys. I like Fitzgerald, Faulkner, and Hemingway". The sincerity in his voice matched the quotes recited from each author's work. If he had memorized all this literature just to look good to a book editor, she was, indeed, impressed. Moreover, if James was just this smart, then Abby was doubly impressed, and had to contain her surprise when she learned he had graduated from the University of North Carolina the year before she earned her degree from Emory.

Maybe James Wilcox was not such a redneck, after all. It seemed he was both smart and attractive, but Abby was not ready to classify James as a "twofer" just yet. She still had too many unanswered questions; like, why was such a smart guy content to work as a deputy sheriff in Rose County, North

Carolina? Abby was not ready to ask that question on a first date. *A first date?* Could that thought mean she was anticipating a second date? Yes she was.

When James pulled his car up to the parsonage, they sat for another hour listening to the radio and talking about music. He explained the importance of a dance called the "shag" and the difference between Carolina beach music, which according to James was "real beach music, and the Beach Boys sound. Abby thought it all, the music and the dance, seemed pretty much like what she saw and heard everywhere else. Still, picturing James on the dance floor made her smile.

He was easy to like and the evening had been nice. James had only asked the usual first date things, Abby's likes and dislikes, hobbies and such. He had not dwelled on her job as an editor and there was certainly no mention of Jessica Cline. As they walked to the front door, Abby began to feel the whole night had been a waste of time. Had she fallen into a trap of her own making? Had the Deputy out-smarted the FBI agent? Did he know why she had really gone out with him? Suddenly she felt like the pawn in a weird game of chess.

A goodnight kiss at the front door completed the saccharine-sweet night. When James asked her out again, her confidence returned. *Check Mate!*

The next evening the war room was busy once again. They reviewed and listed reports of each officer's findings on the morning of the murder. A second board with the heading CRIME SCENE stood next to the one with Jessica's rap sheet. The list read:

- Nude body found, facedown, seventeen inches off the pavement, her left arm and shoulder resting on the embankment, right arm and ankle tucked under her torso.
- Thirty-seven separate stab wounds covered her body. Number thirty-eight lacked approximately six centimeters before total decapitation.
- Medical examiner's reports indicate cause of death was a severed carotid artery. Blood clotting time tests prove other stab wounds were inflicted before the fatal blows.
- Victim's clothing was found scattered across a 100 ft. perimeter of open field. Fifteen tears in her clothing matched specific wounds to the body.
- Time of death was between 4:00 and 4:45 AM.
- There were no witnesses. Residents of the nearest house, about fifty yards away were asleep. Their pit bull, Harley, did not bark.
- Three cigarette butts were found at the crime scene. Two contained the victim's DNA and the other contained DNA from both the victim and the killer. Hilburn Sizemore voluntarily provided his DNA. He was not a match.

"Well, guys, that's it." Abby dusted the chalk from her palms and stepped back to review her handiwork. "And", she added. "That's enough for tonight. Tomorrow, we'll review the investigator's findings... look at everyone they interviewed but, this time, we'll try to read them from a different pont of view."

Noting the disappointed look from Tom, she reminded them that they should take their time so as not to miss any detail.

"Aren't you forgetting to tell us something?" Rachel asked.

"Yes," Tom chimed in. "What about your date? How did it go?"

"You guys amaze me." Abby had prepared for this question. "I have to take my time with this… can't just ask the guy about the case without raising suspicions. We're going out again Sunday so I'm sure I can fish for information then."

Tom nodded in agreement to Abby's response.

Abby pretended not to notice Rachel's look of skepticism.

The next day, Abby tried not to dwell on her upcoming second date with James choosing, instead, to set up the war room for another round of fact checking. Reaching down into one of the boxes of newspaper clippings, Abby pulled out a photo of Jessica printed on the day she died. Tom had said it was the most recent snapshot that Myra Cline could find at the time, taken about a year before Jessica's death.

Abby smoothed out the wrinkles, pinned it to the frame of the board, and stood back studying the victim's face as it stared back at her. Even through the grainy newsprint of the snapshot, Jessica's smile looked disingenuous, even forced, and her eyes held a hauntingly empty stare towards the lens. Abby tried to take her own advice and not read too much into a one-dimensional image. Still, she could not contain the negative feelings she had for the photographer snapping that picture. She studied the blurry background, a beach or lakefront. Jessica could have posed for it anywhere. Not being familiar with the area, Abby had no idea whether or not it was a local setting.

The longer she stared, the more she wondered. Who took that picture? If she could reverse the camera's lens would she, perhaps, be looking at Jessica's killer? Was it possible that the same hands holding the camera to take that picture belonged to the person who held the knife that Halloween morning?

For two days, the friends spent every available minute in the war room diagramming a profile of people known to be close to the victim. They posted every police report, investigative interview note, media transcript, and newspaper copy they had gathered. They added every available photograph to the board.

The ability to put a face with each narrative was a helpful profiler's tool. Although still considered to be freshly out of the Academy at Quantico, Abby had worked with veteran agents long enough to pick up many tricks of the trade. She loved the process of solving crimes and aspired to one day become a proficient profiler. Still, she knew if word got back to the Bureau that she was working on an unauthorized case, her career might be over. No matter how much she loved her friends, she had to be careful not to give away her true occupation.

Well, that date did not go as planned. Abby poured herself a cup of coffee in hopes the caffeine would ease the dull ache in in her right temple. Oversleeping had not helped and when she pulled back the window curtain over the sink the sunlight stabbed at her eyes. According to the clock on the stove, it was almost ten o'clock but the parsonage was quiet. That meant Rachel and Tom were already out. *Thank goodness.* Abby was not ready to discuss her date with anyone yet. She still had to sort last night out for herself.

No doubt, being with James had been great but Abby was becoming concerned that their original plan had backfired—and it was all her fault. Now, she felt guilty—but for what? Could it be that she had forgotten she was dating James just to gain information? No, that was not it. Abby felt guilty because, although she knew better, last night she had put her friends and all thoughts of helping them solve a murder, completely out of her mind. Instead, last night reminded Abby, in the most wonderful way, of the intimacy she had been missing.

From a setting that looked to be straight from a romance novel, James introduced her to Clark Lake. He had said it was his way of showing her there was, indeed, a spot in Rose County quieter than the little community of Eden Falls. *Deliverance* was all she could think of when she saw a "No Trespassing" sign as they turned off the main road and entered the dark dense woods via a one-lane path.

"Don't worry," James teased. "No one's going to shoot us. This land belongs to me."

Abby had a scenic five-minute ride through the woods to digest James' nonchalant explanation of how the dirt road they were on, as well as Clark Lake and its surrounding eight hundred acres, truly belonged to him. Part of an original British land grant, the area had been kept in the family since the 1690's. "After three hundred years, this is all that's left," James said, adding that he was determined to keep these last "few" acres to honor the memory of his late father.

It was a seldom-traveled road, just a one-lane path. Had

it not been for the well-maintained split rail fence running along both sides, it could have been mistaken for a trail used by an occasional hiker or, more often, deer and other wildlife foraging through the pines. Dogwood trees and azaleas marched along the fence, laden to perfection with huge clusters of red, pink and white blooms. Birds perched along the rails of the fence, like a sentry, squawking at the passing vehicle in obvious protection of their nests hidden nearby.

Finally, the lake came into view and in the distance, barely visible at first, a cabin partially hidden on the hill. As they circled the lake, the mirror-smooth surface reflected a canopy of tall pines. Taking in the beauty of Clark Lake, Abby could not help but think this was the closest thing to the Garden of Eden on earth she could imagine – and James owned it all.

From the car window, Abby saw hummingbird feeders hanging from the massive porch. A hungry flock dive-bombed each other, ignoring human intrusion, seeking and hitting each bull's eye full of dripping red nectar with the skill and precision of trained fighter pilots.

"How often do you come out here?" She noticed how clean and well maintained the place looked.

"I practically live here this time of year." As James opened the car door for Abby, he pointed to her feet. "Sorry, I should have reminded you to wear comfortable shoes."

"You probably did and I just forgot," Abby lied. She would show James that she could be country, even in heels. Besides, she thought they made her legs look sexy.

"Never mind," he said. "Just lose the shoes and go barefoot if you want."

Apparently, the appeal of stylish footwear was lost on

this man. Abby climbed the steps and turned to take in the view from the massive porch. "This is gorgeous, James."

Usually not a fan of old and rustic, she could not help but be impressed with the unusual style of this cabin. Low-hanging eaves gave cover to the wide porch that wrapped all four sides of the house. The railing was made entirely of bent tree branches, intricately twisted and woven together, without a nail in sight. Its satiny surface looked polished to a semi-gloss finish, enticing Abby to draw her fingers around and through the smooth-as-silk branches and, when she drew her hand near her face; she could smell the forest on her fingertips.

"Yeah, I love it here. I'm lucky to have inherited this place." He ushered Abby inside. "It's been in my family for about 200 years…since English land-grant days. James moved about the room as he talked, opening windows and unlocking the double French doors. Along with a welcome rush of breeze came a glorious view of Clark Lake.

"Just about every generation has improved or updated the property, some way or another. My Grandpa wanted it to stay untouched. Hell, he fought wiring the place for electricity until Dad put his foot down. So…" James flipped the light switch to reveal an updated kitchen. "We got rid of the wood-burning stove."

"I would love to keep it authentic but I've become too soft. This place has great natural ventilation but I like my comfort." He reached for the next wall switch. Fresh air and the sound of ceiling fans began to hum. "There." James turned to survey the room as though looking for something he may have missed.

"It's amazing, James…just beautiful." Between the scenic view and the chirping birds, Abby was in sensory overload. She imagined this must be what Alice experienced when she fell down the rabbit hole.

"How 'bout a beer?" James had moved to the kitchen. "I know it's only one o'clock but you know what Jimmy Buffet says…" he twisted off the cap and handed the bottle to Abby.

She was not much of a beer drinker; she preferred wine. However, here, as with everything else in this setting, preferences did not necessarily fit. She was thirsty and a cold beer sounded great. Tiny beads of cold water ran down the bottle and felt wonderful as they dripped on her left wrist. When she turned the bottle up for a drink, she felt James take her right hand in his.

"So, you're a "leftie", too." James was grinning at her.

Abby looked puzzled until she realized he had noticed she held the beer bottle with her left hand when she drank.

"Yes, you're pretty observant, there, Officer." Abby chuckled but she was, indeed, impressed that he had noticed her recessive trait. Especially, since she had not noticed that James, too, was left-handed.

"Guess we do have something in common after all," Abby teased. As he led her out to the back porch swing.

Abby was mesmerized as James told her about the area, its history, and his attachment to it. Clearly, he seemed to know every inch of the land. He pointed to and gave the generic name of every tree and natural flower visible from the cabin's porch.

"Most of the trees out here are either native or replanted from heirloom seeds. Grandpa planted the cornus lining the driveway… and Dad planted the cornus rubra." Abby was trying not to look as clueless as she felt when James added, "You probably call them Dogwoods in Georgia. And of course, cornus rubra is…"

"Pink dogwoods?" Abby could not help herself. She had to let him know she did know a little bit of Latin, although a very little bit.

"Yes." James seemed to realize he sounded a little pretentious. Still he turned his attention to the wildlife around the lake. He pointed out birds on the opposite side of the lake and could recognize their sounds before they were fully in view. He showed her herons perched on a log in the lake, adding that most people mistook them for cranes. Abby admitted that she did as well. Yes, Abby thought, James knows this place and she could tell how much he loved it.

How divine, she thought. The swing, the setting, the beer…and the company sent a wave of simple comfort through her. It was the first time in ages that she felt completely safe and at peace. The rhythmic back and forth of the swing was in tandem with the glancing sunlight as it danced across the pristine waters of Clark Lake.

James was sliding the near-empty beer bottle from her hand when Abby realized she was about to fall asleep. "Wake up sleepyhead!"

Embarrassed, she followed when he pulled her from the swing and led her towards the door.

"You're bound to be getting hungry. I know I am." He pointed her towards an old tabletop radio before turning to the kitchen. He pulled a tray of cold cuts, cheese, and sliced tomatoes from the fridge, then chips and a loaf of bread.

"Nothing fancy I'm afraid but, maybe, this will do for now." He grinned when he placed a bottle of cabernet and a corkscrew next to two glasses.

Abby turned the huge knobs on the radio through static until she found a strong signal, playing "My Girl". She had found the oldies station and left it there since it had been hard enough to find something static-free. She turned around to face James who handed her a glass of wine and raised his in a toast. "Here's to spending a wonderful day with the most beautiful writer I know."

With the clinking of their glasses in toast, Abby felt more than a little twinge of guilt. "That's a sweet sentiment, James but...you're wrong about me." She looked into his eyes, dreading to tell him the truth. "You've got my occupation wrong."

"What do you mean?" James' smile was gone.

"I'm not a writer." Abby held his gaze a little too long. "I'm a ...book editor." She had chickened out. "That's not quite the same thing." She knew she must tell him the truth—eventually.

"Oh, God, I know that. I'm sorry, Abby." James looked embarrassed at making that silly mistake.

If you only knew, Abby knew this charade must end. She finished her glass of wine and held out the empty for him to refill. "Just half a glass, please." She needed to be sober enough to discuss Jessica Cline.

"You make a great sandwich, Officer." Abby quipped as she placed their empty plates in the sink. "Just when did you prepare all this?" She had been looking around the room noting how pristine everything was, not a speck of dust anywhere.

"Okay, I confess. I came up here early this morning, gave the place a little once-over, and brought up the food and wine... I wasn't about to let you see it in its usual state."

"Well, I'm impressed." Abby smiled and held out her glass for another "half". "This is very good wine. California?"

James held up the bottle and read the label. "Actually, it's made in Georgia. Imagine that. I've never tried it before but I was sure it would be good. Guess you could say it's the second best thing I've found lately that comes from Georgia."

Corny, but she felt a glow that she knew came only partly from the wine. She heard a familiar old song and walked over to turn up the radio volume. Abby closed her eyes and swayed back and forth, losing herself in the moment as the Isley Brothers crooned, "When a Man Loves a Woman". She had no particular reason to like this genre of music but, like everything else she had experienced today, it just felt perfect.

"Dance with me?" James did not wait for her to answer. He took her hand and pulled her close swaying to the rhythm. As she pressed her body against his chest, the song and her feeling seemed to fill the room. He felt good to her. He smelled good to her. Both were senses Abby had felt before, yet not with this intensity.

The song ended but their embrace did not. His hands eased across her hips, brushing the curve of her buttocks before palming her close. His hot breath teased her neck then wafted across her earlobe. He kissed her, softly and when she sighed, she hoped he caught the signal it sent. She hoped his measure of desire met her own.

A sound against the window drew Abby's attention. "It's

117

starting to rain," breathless, she almost panted the words.

"Good," he said. "Making love is always better in the rain." He kissed her deeply then led her into the bedroom.

It was dark when they left the cabin. They said little, but their passion still hung in the air, sweet and heavy. Leaving Clark Lake, just before reaching the main road, James placed the car in park, leaned over and brushed her cheek with his fingertips. "I just want to make sure you are real…that you're not just my perfect dream."

After another lingering kiss, James pulled the car onto the highway. They listened to the same, great, oldies station all the way back to Eden Falls, singing along even when they could not remember the words. It had been a perfect day, Abby thought.

Reality rushed in when James pulled onto Bethel Church Road. What should she tell Rachel and Tom? Not the truth, that was for sure. She could never tell them they never talked about the murder; that she had not even mentioned Jessica Cline's name. She could not even tell them part of the truth, certainly not the part where she spent the whole day drinking and dancing barefoot in James family's cabin. And heaven help her if they knew the whole truth; that she had spent the better part of the day having mad, passionate, animal sex in the woods with a man she had only known a few days. Worst of all, she knew that if given the chance, she would do it again.

A rooster was crowing nearby when Abby slipped out the backdoor the next morning. Getting to the war room before Tom and Rachel awoke was the best way to avoid the breakfast table inquisition about her date with James. With just a few more days before her return to Atlanta, Abby felt pressured to make some decisions about her next move with the case – and James.

She was working with renewed motivation and enthusiasm when Rachel stuck her head in the door with an apology. The hospital had called her to cover for a nurse with a sick child. *Thank God!* Now, if Tom would stay out of her way, maybe Abby could think clearly enough to know what to do next.

Three months ago, Abby had never heard of Jessica Cline nor James Wilcox. Now, all she thought of were these two people. Moreover, she was unsure of what her next step would be to resolve either problem.

As she pulled out of the driveway to meet James, Abby promised herself this would not be a repeat of their previous date. She was headed towards Frank's, the only bar in town as James pointed out to her when they headed to Clark Lake a few days before.

She knew he had been confused when she asked to meet there since he remembered their conversation about the place. Frank's, he said, was notorious for being a hard-core biker bar, usually full of liquored up rednecks ready to fight. His description of the place made her chuckle when he said, "If a rumor is whispered inside Frank's, it will sweep throughout town and back so fast that everyone will know your business before you can reach your car in the parking lot". Abby had anticipated James' surprise when she said she wanted to meet there and had three reasons for doing so.

First, she wanted the locals to see them together, in case someone already knew they were dating. Whether good or bad, that little bit of street cred could come in handy later.

Second, it was time to tell James the truth about her occupation and her real reason for being here. If he stormed out after her confession, at least she would be able to have another drink before returning to her tee-totaling friends back at the Baptist church.

Finally, meeting at Frank's would keep Abby safe from her emotions and the temptation to return to Clark Lake, the place she seemed to lose all her left-brain thinking.

James was waiting when Abby drove up.

"Are you sure this is where you want to meet?"

"James! Are you ashamed to be seen with me?" She was being facetious but still, awaited his reply.

"Now, Abby…really. You know what I mean." He stammered a little. "I mean, you'd better be prepared to hear gossip, out of context I might add, by tomorrow morning."

"Let them talk. I don't care." Then she added, "Do you?"

"You just don't understand small towns, Abby."

To Abby, that comment stung a bit but she had no time to worry if James thought she was a city girl snob. That was a fight for another day — she hoped. For now, she stifled hurt feelings and suggested they go inside for a drink.

They took a booth near the back and ordered a Bloody Mary for him and a Screwdriver for Abby.

"So? What's up?" He asked.

"James", she stopped and took a gulp of her drink. "Wow — that's…" she grimaced.

"Too much vodka?" James began looking around for the server.

"No, too much O.J." Abby stopped him and laughed.

With the mood lightened, Abby began her speech. "James, I need to tell you something and wanted to meet you somewhere other than your house or the cabin. Both places have too many distractions — especially the cabin." She knew she was beginning to ramble so she downed the rest of her drink.

"Abby, I'm trying to make sense of what you are saying." The wrinkles in James' forehead deepened. "But, why can't you tell me — whatever it is you have to tell me— at Tom's place?"

Abby saw he was getting irritated.

"You're right — we will — go back to the parsonage, I mean. I'm sorry, but I need to confess something first — and I really needed a drink to bolster my nerves."

As James motioned to the server for drink refills, a realization seemed to cover his face.

"Are you trying to tell me you don't want to see me again?" His demeanor changed and his voice rose. "I know you're from the big city of Atlanta — four whole hours away. Nevertheless, I do have a map and a college degree! I can figure out how to get there."

"Whoa, Deputy! What I have to tell you has nothing to do with us." Abby reached over and took his hand. "Well, maybe a little — but mostly," Abby swallowed hard. "I just want to prepare you for what is going on in the church basement."

When the server delivered their drinks to the table, Abby

hushed. Thankfully, hers was stronger this time. She hoped his was, too.

"Good Lord, Abby, what are you talking about?" James reached for his Bloody Mary and downed it.

They noticed the bar had become a little too quiet, so they finished the cocktails and decided to continue their talk in the car. For Abby, the drinks seemed to have hit their mark. Her nerves were calm and she was ready to confess her transgressions.

Sitting in her car, Abby told James the truth, from confessing her real occupation to the fact that Rachel asked her to Eden Falls because of the Jessica Cline murder. She even told him of Tom's growing obsession with the case.

"James, Rachel is my best friend…"

"So, you're really acting as a double agent?" James interrupted. "That was your reason for dating me?" He leaned away from Abby and pressed his back against the car door.

"Yes – at first." Abby would not lie to James again. "When your best friend needs your help – well, what was I supposed to do?"

Abby told James the story of the morning he drove up to the church and nearly discovered her in the clandestine war room. "Although I couldn't see you, I immediately liked two things about you that day," Abby leaned closer to him as she spoke. "The compassion in your voice and the perfect shine on your shoes. When we finally met and spent time together, my attraction to you grew into something stronger."

James listened in silence as Abby confessed her reasons for lying to him for so long.

"If I didn't have real feelings for you I would still be

pretending to be a book editor. If I didn't care for you, I would never admit all this." She tried to choke back tears.

Abby talked and cried until she got it all out. "I am so sorry," she said. Then she took a deep breath, and waited for James to respond.

James wiped the tears from her cheek and pulled her close. "I love you," he said.

Abby realized she was now sober, though emotionally drained. If she had heard him right, she hoped James was sober, too.

James followed Abby back to the parsonage where Rachel expressed surprise at seeing them back so early and confused when Abby asked for Tom to join them at the kitchen table.

"I want James to see the war room," Abby stated, then began to explain why James should be included in their investigation.

Before she had said a dozen words, Tom stood and kicked the kitchen chair away from the table, grabbed Abby by the elbow and guided her into the den.

"Are you out of your mind?" Tom pushed Rachel back, ignoring her attempt to stop him.

Abby knew Tom would be skeptical at first, but she never expected this visceral a reaction.

"Abby, this guy is a Deputy Sheriff – loyal to the very agency who has given up on finding the killer, and…"

"Wait," Abby stopped him in mid-sentence with her raised voice. "Please, hear me out. I think James can help us. I only have a couple days left before I go back to Atlanta. I thought you would welcome his help; but if you're ready to give up, that's fine, too."

Tom glanced back at Rachel who took her husband's hand and stroked his arm, lovingly.

"Honey, why don't we go to the church basement and let James see all our hard work? Abby's right. We're running out of time." Rachel's soothing voice seemed to bring Tom back to a state of reason.

For the first time, Abby saw, firsthand, the battles Rachel had been fighting the past months. Tom displayed a different personality from the one Abby knew in college and it scared her. However, instead of scaring her off, Abby was more committed than ever to do everything necessary to help her friends.

Tom apologized to James, justifying his outburst with the reminder that the congregation would be outraged at this use of the church basement.

"Whatever it takes, Preacher." James calmly reached over to shake Tom's hand. Then placing Abby's in his, James added, "And, yes, Abby has told me everything."

Switching on the light in the war room produced images so vivid they shocked even a seasoned deputy such as James. It was unlike any crime investigation room he had ever seen, at least; nothing like the one downtown. Tom walked him around the room, slowly, as James surveyed the bulletin boards, covered in notes, pictures and newspaper clippings, which stood alongside chalkboards covered, top to bottom, in handwritten scribble. the room looked like an enormous eclectic art project. He paused to examine, more closely, the state-of-the-art desktop computer. A fax machine and huge printer sat beside cases of paper, tractor-fed into the machines, poised to spit out snake-like pages into an empty box, standing at the ready. A new laptop computer sat, efficiently placed near two, side-by-side telephones. James took a three-hundred and sixty degree canvas around the room, stopping his spin in front of Tom.

"Damn! We don't have this much crap downtown. This is pretty amazing!"

"Yes, isn't it great? We've been working down here for two months now." Tom beamed. Proudly, assuming the deputy's statement to be a compliment.

"Two months?" James glanced at Abby.

"Actually, Tom's counting from the time of my first visit. Remember? I told you about the morning I first saw you. Or, at least, your shoes." She started to giggle but stopped when saw that Tom was no longer grinning.

"Like I said, Tom, I've told James everything, including the morning you talked with him outside the basement window."

Letting a sheepish grin slip, Tom responded, "Oh... right, right. Well, sorry about that lie, James. It's just that you caught me off guard that day and I said the first thing that came to my mind."

"No problem, Tom." James attention was elsewhere Abby could tell.

She could tell he was still in shock, still trying to take in all the data that nearly overwhelmed the space. Abby watched James as he studied the enlarged crime scene photos taped to the walls and stacks of newspaper clippings on the table. Every few feet he would stop and glance back at the computer technology in the corner of the room. She wondered if James questioned their procedures or just the appropriateness of the environment.

Rachel pointed to the first alphabet-adorned chalkboard and suggested that Tom and Abby explain their process. "The clock's ticking, remember?" She directed James to a chair and added. "I'll put on the coffee."

For the next hour, the three friends explained the process and their findings to date. James only interrupted when they began to talk over each other or when they left out parts that they all knew so well it was easy to forget that James had not been there the whole time.

After a two-hour presentation, James seemed genuinely impressed. Abby was pleased that the evening had gone so well and was thrilled at his offer to help with the case. She had not forgotten James earlier proclamation.

A cool three AM fog enveloped them as they leaned against the car and kissed goodbye. Slipping her arms beneath his jacket and around his waist, Abby held James tight and whispered one last confession.

"I love you, too.

It was easy to get an appointment with Senator Connors — almost too easy, Abby thought. She was prepared for him to hang up the phone when she called the day before, especially when she told him who she was and why she wanted to meet with him. He not only agreed to today's meeting but sounded happy about it. And that made Abby a little nervous.

Since coming clean to James about her true occupation, Abby no longer worried about hiding the truth. That gave her an added sense of security and, she hoped it might elicit a little newfound respect from the locals. They were bound to be a little intimidated by an FBI agent. And, as long as the war room stayed hidden and secret, they were safe.

Even in the slow and sleepy south, news travels fast and Abby was certain that the hotline between Raleigh and Eden Falls lit up as soon as her call to Senator Connors ended. By now, he had done a background check on Abby, for sure, which is why she had cleared the visit with the bosses at her Atlanta office as soon as she decided to make the visit to Connors' legislative office in the state capitol. Most likely, he realized Abby knew about Ashton's relationship with Jessica Cline; might even have suspected she had information about the baby. And, if he was like every other politician she had met, he was already in "damage control" mode—a political figure's ability to answer a question without giving any meaningful information. The more years they held office the more practiced they became.

The drive to Raleigh took less than an hour and finding the State Legislature was a breeze. The state capitol looked to be a pleasant old city, neither too big nor too small, and without the traffic nightmare of Atlanta's gridlocked streets. If she had time after her meeting, maybe she would look up the local Bureau office, just for the heck of it.

"Welcome to Raleigh, Miz Rials." Senator William Connors walked towards her with his hand outstretched in the every-ready, over-practiced, good ol' boy greeting. A fixed grin that looked too big for his face seemed about as sincere as his rehearsed greeting, "so nice to meet you."

Abby could not deny that Connors was distinguished

127

looking, a charmer who managed to make even his professionally whitened, toothy smile seem genuine. His dark hair peppered with a perfect touch of gray at the temples, was barbered into a youthful style, just long enough to belie his age of sixty-eight. As he invited her into his office and offered her a seat, she caught a subtle waft of his cologne. It smelled expensive. Then she noticed his tie, probably woven from pure silk and finished with a perfectly tied knot. He leaned across the massive mahogany desk, attentive to her every word and giving the impression of lending full support to her visit. Senator Connors proved himself worthy of the office he held.

"Thank you, Senator for agreeing to see me. I'll try not to take up much of your time but I want to ask about your son, Ashton." Abby continued before he could interject. "It's pretty clear that he and Jessica Cline had been close for quite some time." Abby noted Connors' slight shoulder tensing. Still, she kept talking. "I know that Ashton has been cleared as a suspect in her murder but thought he may have said something to you about the other people in her life."

With a negative nod of his head, Connors finally spoke. "No, he never said much to me about the girl."

"Senator, did Ashton ever talk about marrying Jessica?"

Connors pushed away from his desk and turned his chair around to face the window.

The plush leather chair gently rocked back and forth, its occupant's back to Abby.

"Miz Rials," he spoke slowly, drawing out each syllable. "Just who has sent you here?" Then, he twirled his chair back to face her once again. "And, just what do you want?" His was smile was gone.

"As I said on the phone, when I was visiting friends here in March, I was made aware of the case by Reverend Tom Kirby. His wife, Rachel has been my friend since childhood. Tom, as a concerned citizen as well as the minister who delivered Jessica's eulogy, asked if I could look into the case since the killer is still at large. While I am an agent with the FBI, I'm just a rookie—still learning. I'm doing this strictly on my own time. Just want to help out — as a courtesy to my friends."

Abby knew better than to lie to the Senator about her identity since he had, most likely, checked her out as soon as he hung up the phone from her first call. Moreover, the small town rumor mill was bound to be in full operation back in Rose County. Most likely, Connors' question had been a test to see if he could trust her and, for now, she needed his trust. Judging by the softening in his voice and demeanor, Abby must have passed.

"Miz...may I call you Abby?"

She nodded.

"Let me tell you why I agreed to meet with *you*." He cleared his throat and continued. "My son, Ashton, has been a challenge for me all his life. He drove his mother to drink, His actions and my wife's alcoholism eventually led to her death...my dear wife..." His voice and thoughts seemed to trail off until he caught himself. "But I can't blame my son completely. He's sick. I know that."

Through quivering lips, he added. "Ashton's not a killer. I am certain of that. I have agreed to talk with you in hopes of, like you, finding the truth—and the killer. Until then, there will always be those that suspect my son had something to do with her demise. Till then, the Connors name can never be truly cleared."

"Do you know how we might find her killer?" Abby asked.

"I've told the authorities everything I know—answered all their questions. If I knew something—anything, well of course, I would tell them."

Spoken like a true politician, she thought. Abby knew he wasn't telling everything. She needed to end this cat and mouse game and get his attention. She stood, ready to leave but turned back to Connors who seemed relieved the interview was over.

"Senator, I know that Jessica gave birth to a baby boy in 1988. In addition, I know he was placed for adoption. Was Ashton the baby's father?" Abby took a quick breath and continued. "Is Jessica's baby your grandson, Mr. Connors?"

She had deliberately called him Mr. rather than Senator, subtle intimidation Abby hoped would level the playing field a bit. She knew it had worked when she saw the look of surprise on Connors' face.

"It is my political duty to help my constituents when called upon to do so." He began. "Since Jessica was my son's friend, I merely helped the Cline family with their daughter's problem."

"What does that mean? Does it mean you are aware that Ashton fathered this child, Senator?" Abby's question remained on point.

He cleared his throat, slipping easily back into politician mode.

"As I said, I don't deny helping this young lady with her

situation. Things were done with the best interest of everyone in mind—especially that of the child. I might add that I have never discussed this subject with anyone other than the Clines. It's a private matter. I would not want to embarrass Jessica's family, nor my son."

"Or you political reputation?" Abby added.

Connors fired back, "I don't see how something that happened years ago is relevant to finding a killer. It has nothing to do with the murder. As for the child, no – I do not consider him my grandson." His voice level rose, picking up strength as he continued. "A wonderful, caring family adopted him and I relinquished my title as grandparent at that point."

The Senator told how Ashton had come to him with the news that Jessica was pregnant and they asked for his help. Recognizing they were unable to care for a child was probably the only healthy decision they ever made as a couple. Connors met with Theo Cline who agreed to an out-of-state birth and adoption.

"Untraceable" he said. "We were told no one would ever find out. Yet, here we are. You seem to have uncovered the little bastard quite easily."

Abby could not hide her shock at the Senator's choice of words and, for a moment was speechless. Suddenly, Connors remembered he was late for a meeting and apologized at having cut their visit short. The adoption, he said, was in the distant past, therefore a closed subject. Expressing sorrow that today's visit was fruitless and reminding Abby, he was always available to answer more pertinent questions, Connors reached out to shake her hand. Then, in a move as skilled as a practiced dance step, his right palm eased to the small of her back, gently nudging her towards the door. He continued spinning political bullshit, talking through his toothy grin, until he had waltzed her out the back door of his office.

Abby realized that she was just kicked out of the Senator's office. Politely and expertly done, but kicked out just the same. And for a moment Abby thought she might have felt the sensation of his palm as it slipped from her back and lingered a little too long against her buttocks. The woman in her did not have time to feel violated since her investigator persona rejoiced at her discovery.

Her plan to find and visit the Bureau's Raleigh office would have to wait. Dictating into a voice-activated recorder as she drove, she tried to remember every detail of her visit with Connors. At her mention of the adoption, Abby had struck a nerve with the Senator. Still, not sure of how it tied into the murder, it was a new clue, an important clue, one that connected Theo Cline and the Senator on a different level.

Abby could hardly wait to get back to the war room.

10.

May 12, 1999
Sen. William Connors, Jr.

The Senator watched from his office window as Abby Rials' BMW pulled out of the main Capital Building parking lot. He could not deny that it was shocking to learn this young woman had uncovered information he thought safely hidden from the public. This was a family matter, no reason for any FBI involvement. So why? Had someone breached a confidence?

It had been nearly four years since he had worried about anyone discovering existence of the boy. Surely, he was no longer a threat to his political career. He had even stopped worrying about how many people knew about it. He used to be concerned that Jessica, while under the influence or while attempting to buy drugs, would say too much to the wrong person. That had been the only potential political threat Jessica Cline had ever posed to the Senator. Since her death, Connors had been able to put the adoption out of his mind; one problem eliminated, he thought. However, today's visit from "little miss FBI" was troubling. How could she have stumbled onto information he thought so well protected?

He sank into his chair and reached over to the photograph

of his boys, displayed proudly on the corner of his desk. He picked up the picture, taken the same day as the large family portrait hanging in his office conference room. Both pictures belied the chaos of family dysfunction they all endured. Taken only a few months before his wife, Rosalyn, or Pinky as family and close friends called her, died of liver failure. It was their last family picture. Her death was near, anyone could see it, even the retouched photo could not hide, completely, jaundice in her eyes. The Senator never fully recovered from losing his beloved Pinky. Petite and stylish, she had been the perfect politician's wife. She loved to entertain and, as everyone knew, she loved her cocktails. So, no one was surprised at the postmortem diagnosis of cirrhosis when she died at age sixty. That is, no one except Senator Connors who, secretly, blamed his sons; Trey, the doctor, for not catching his mother's liver disease and Ashton for driving is mother to drink. Connors' fingers caressed the picture frame. What did he ever do to deserve such an awful family?

No, William Connors, Jr. was not sure what had gone wrong in his younger son's life to lead him down such a path of self-destruction. Certainly, his firstborn had never been that kind of problem. Will Connors, III, Trey to friends and family, was a successful physician with a flourishing practice in Eden Falls. Both Trey and his father were the pillars of society.

Ashton, like Trey, should have been a high achiever. Both son's intelligence test scores were equally impressive. Just two years separated the boys in age but miles stood between them in character and lifestyle. The more successful Trey became, the further astray Ashton seemed to

134

drift. When Pinky died, the Senator's attempts to control Ashton's wild ways proved impossible.

When his younger son's antics became intolerable, the Senator made a very public display of disowning him, throwing him out of the family mansion in the presence of the housekeeping staff and the gardener. But that incident had been just for show as the Senator continued to enable Ashton's addictive behavior in private. After two failed attempts at out-of-state inpatient rehabilitation for alcoholism, Connors gave up.

A little house, about three miles outside of town, away from complaining neighbors, seemed the perfect environment. Connors purchased it for Ashton as a solution for his son as well as a method to help his political career. Trey managed his brother's medical care while hired help kept the floors swept, groceries stocked, and weeds trimmed at Ashton's little cottage tucked at the end of a dirt path on Old Post Road. This arrangement worked well for the Connors men – most of the time. Senator Connors knew Ashton had dodged many bullets, both medically and legally, over the past couple of years. He wondered if his enabling should have ended sooner.

11.

May 23, 1999
James Wilcox

I t had been less than 24 hours since he saw Abby's little convertible exit onto Interstate 95, taking her back to Atlanta. James had followed her, police escort style, to the county line, partly as a courtesy but, mostly, because he wanted to be near her as long as possible. That was silly, he knew, but did not care.

They were together until late the night before; planning their next steps in what had become a mystery they vowed to solve. The unconventional band of sleuths now numbered four and each brought their own brand of expertise to the table. Each had their own personal reasons to solve the murder, too. Tom wanted to honor Jessica Cline's memory, Rachel wanted to protect Tom's emotional wellbeing, Abby wanted to help her friends, and James wanted to do his job. Oh yes, and then there was the love thing.

The plan was for Abby to return to her job and request a transfer to the Raleigh branch of the Bureau. Abby told James her request should go smoothly.

"Agents rarely requested transfer out of the Atlanta office, especially to a sleepy place like Raleigh. Most might even consider it a demotion." Abby bit her lip and gave a wincing glance to James. "Sorry," she added.

James was not offended. He knew Raleigh would not be an exciting place for an action-hungry FBI agent. Rather he was impressed with all he had seen the night before in the church basement and the dedication of the amateur investigators.

His romantic interest in Abby was just part of the reason James was excited about the events of the past few days—a big part, yes—but only one part. He wanted to bring the killer to justice, too. James' childhood memories of Jessica Cline were nearly as clear as the shock he felt the day Hilburn Sizemore discovered her body, the least he could do would be to lend his expertise to the effort.

After meeting the previous night, each team member left with an assignment. Tom would move his desk closer to the window in his office. From there, he had a clear view of the entrance to the church basement. Keeping the war room safe from prying eyes or anyone getting too close was the minister's assignment for now.

Rachel would use her status as nursing supervisor at Rose County Medical Center to delve into medical records detailing Ashton Connors' hospitalization on the day of Jessica's murder.

Abby would return to Atlanta and submit her paperwork for a transfer. The night before, she shared with James that she knew this would come as a surprise to her boss but her gut told her it was the right choice. Abby hoped there would be no glitch with her request. James hoped the same.

Now, James was on his way to work in the annex building

of the Rose County Courthouse. For once, he was happy to be working away from most coworkers in his department. When first told his office would be in the historic courthouse until renovations were complete in the current building, James was not happy. Just two other deputies worked there, along with some of the tax office personnel. The old, circa 1900, building was a dirty, mold-infested brick structure that once held two courtrooms, municipal offices on the first floor. The historic Rose County jail took up the top two floors. James temporary workspace was, in fact, the jailer's old office, and his only storage room was an empty jail cell, bars still intact.

James had not minded the move, at first. He had even volunteered to occupy one of the old turn of the century era offices, with fifteen-foot ceilings and massive windows. Then it became clear that parts of the old courthouse, including the entire first floor, contained dangerous asbestos. The expense of removing the cancer-causing material nearly shelved the move until the second floor was found clear of carcinogens. Apparently, with everything made of steel, the jail had no need for use of hazardous building material. Problem solved, James soon moved into his office on the second floor. *How nice.*

James fumed for the entire two weeks it took to clean and repair enough of the second floor for county employees to install computers and phone lines. However, when County maintenance removed the cell's door, cutting through steel bolts & hinges with blowtorches, James had to admit, it was not so bad. The metal bunks served as great shelving and could hold tons of boxes full of old files awaiting transfer to microfilm.

Turned out, the old jail was a good place to work, too. It was quiet and when he needed a break, he would pour himself a cup of coffee and stretch his legs by exploring the massive building. Long-abandoned jail cells lined the dark second-floor hallways. The thick steel bars and the deliberate closeness of their spacing, was a strange contrast to the cell doors, which now stood wide open. They looked almost welcoming, like cabins on a cruise ship awaiting their guests. Inside each, graffiti covered the walls. There were names dates, proclamations, curse words, even poems of misery and regret. To James, the most amazing sight was the artwork, some of it exquisitely done, left behind by some of Rose County's former "guests".

Strange to admit, but James knew he might just miss this place when he moved back into his real-world office in a few months.

"Come on in and pull up a chair, James." Sheriff Sanders wondered why his favorite deputy needed to see him first thing on Monday morning. "What's going on? Don't get to see you much since your office is all the way across the street, now."

"Oh, nothing special. Just wanted to check in and run something by you." James had practiced this part.

"Have a seat." Omar gestured for James to close the door.

"I was just wondering if we have anything new on the Cline murder." James did not look at Sanders, but continued. "Any new hunches? You know — just gut feelings. Or do you think this one's gone cold?"

139

"Cold, for sure. Why? Have you heard something?"

"Oh, no." James shrugged and shot his boss a nonchalant glance. "I saw her brother, Wesley, the other day and I was, you know, just thinking about her." James lied. "You think it's time we looked into it again?"

The Sheriff did not seem enthusiastic but was about to answer when his telephone rang. "Sheriff Sanders speaking... Hold on." He covered the receiver with this hand and glanced over at his visitor. "Why don't you do a little work on it, if you want to and have time? Let me know if you come up with anything."

"Sure, I'll do that." That was all James needed to hear.

"Oh, wait a minute." The Sheriff stopped him. "That killer is long gone by now. We already know pretty much what happened. So don't waste a lot of time on this case, you hear me?"

James acknowledged the Sheriff with a nod and took off, back to the musty smell of his temporary office. For the first time, he wondered if his boss had really given up on finding Jessica Cline's killer. Had he, too, bought into the theory of the transient killer? James never thought his boss would take the easy way out or, worse still, be influenced by a payoff. Before he let his imagination run wild or suspect the worst about Omar or his coworkers, he would do a little research of his own.

He found the boxes containing notes from the early stages of the investigation closer than he realized. They sat nearby, just one cell over from his own makeshift storage room. An omen, James thought. For once, he was happy to spend time in his dungeon-like office, away from prying eyes and today, as luck would have it, all was quiet on the law enforcement front. He had plenty of time to review the case once again.

"Do you think there will be any problem making copies for us?"

Abby was happy to hear James' voice and the phone call was the first time they had spoken since she left early the day before. They had agreed to try not to talk during work hours. No need to raise suspicion at either work place.

"No. I will copy anything that you have not already seen. Actually, so far I've not found much you don't already have posted in the war room." James only wanted to talk about how much he missed her but he knew they had to get business out of the way before Abby would relax enough to whisper anything intimate.

She had put in her request for transfer, which she said, raised no eyebrows with her co-workers.

"The only response I got from Agent Tillis was that he didn't see where a move would be a problem." Abby sighed. "I can't lie that I'm a little disappointed. I suppose I just thought I was needed more than I am here in Atlanta."

"Well, my response is the opposite. I'm thrilled!" James was sincere. "They just don't know how valuable you are down there in Atlanta. When you come back up here, I won't let you get away from me that easily."

The small talk soon drifted into pillow talk, something that would become a nightly ritual and one that would make the next few weeks bearable for the new lovers. They savored the nightly talks, making plans for a future that would begin with solving a murder.

The next two weeks were quiet in the Sheriff's office. Apparently, Rose County was back to the familiar slow pace of rural life and, aside from a two-day cleanup from an overturned truck full of hogs headed to market, there was very little to break the monotony. Four hundred squealing pigs headed in all directions can be hard to catch. It was as though they knew their destiny, so they gave it all they had to try to get away. James felt a bit sorry for them but, hog farming was big business around this part of North Carolina, and the livestock's owner was grateful to those who helped get them to the slaughterhouse. The whole fiasco had been the only excitement in the county of late, even attracting the news media. James' hard work was even memorialize with a front-page picture of him in yesterday's *Tribune,* chasing down an escaped hog. The caption read, "A Good Deputy Always Catches the Swine."

Before pinning it to the bulletin board over his desk, James faxed the picture to Abby, knowing she would get a good laugh out of it. Then he sat back, staring at the clipping and thinking, *how odd* — the same place that is so quiet that runaway pigs are front-page news could completely ignore an unsolved murder among its neighbors. Somehow, this just felt wrong to James.

He picked up an AP picture of Jessica Cline, printed the day after her murder and stared at the one-dimensional image. What did she feel as she died? James wondered. Was it pure pain or was there room to experience fear while she was being hacked to pieces? He thought back over the years to grade school, watching her board the school bus with her brothers. He remembered how she looked every morning,

142

her blonde hair bouncing in ringlets from the ponytails fixed over each ear. The reason he noticed her was that the bus driver would yell for her to hurry up.

"Come on kid," he would shout. "I've got three more stops — For Christ sake! Let's go!" Every day it was the same pattern and it always took her the same amount of time to climb the school bus steps. You would have thought the driver's job of getting to school each day, rested on the shoulders of that little girl. James remembered that no one ever helped little Jessica up the steps. Not the bus driver, not Wesley, nor Nolan.

I did not help her either, James thought. Fact was, even if he was tempted to offer such help, he would have looked like a sissy and no respectable ten year-old boy wanted to be a sissy. Perhaps, that is why this was the only clear memory of the victim that stands out in James' mind. Even though, they attended the same school and rode the same bus for most of those years, Jessica Cline would live in James' memory as the little girl who always made them late for school every day.

Could this be one reason James was so anxious to help with the case? Surely, guilt over something so trivial, something that took place so long ago and that he really had no direct hand in, would not factor into his adult decisions. No, James knew that Abby Rials was his reason to get involved. He had fallen for her, fast and hard and he would help no matter who the victim, just to work alongside Abby. Still, there could be nothing wrong with soothing his conscience a little bit along the way.

12.

May 30, 1999
Abby Rials

For someone who disliked clutter and took pride in living well with just the basics, Abby was starting to feel like a hoarder. There was so much stuff to pack. Empty boxes sat in each room, awaiting her decision of what to take versus what to toss or give away, and it was becoming an overwhelming task.

She was trying to do too much, too fast and she began to cry when a too-tall stack of books toppled onto her foot. Her tears were from both physical and emotional pain. For the first time in her life, she had made a life-changing decision, totally, by herself. It was a big step to move from Atlanta to North Carolina and the thought frightened her.

Atlanta had always been her home. Even after her parents' death, her grandmother cared for her just a few miles from the only other home she knew. Granny devoted the rest of her life to raising Abby. She was always there to provide love, reserved though it was, along with a strict upbringing and the best education money could buy. She was strong and self-sufficient, traits Granny worked hard to instill into her only grandchild.

Abby's earliest childhood memory was of hearing, at age five, that she was an orphan. The death of her parents in a plane crash was a tragedy. For most children, fear and sadness would be all they could gain from such trauma. Not so for Abby. Instead, Granny's words to Abby on that awful day stood to shape her life and guide her, still.

"Now, child, I know you're hurting. I am too. But we've got each other — and that's all we need." She could still hear the gentle squeak of Granny's rocker as her voice softened and settled deep in Abby's memory. "Just you remember — you will never have anything worse than this happen to you — me neither but, Rials women are tough. Remember, you can handle anything on your own. Anything — you hear me child?"

That became Granny's mantra with every change in in Abby's life. Boarding the bus to summer camp at age ten, her ninth-grade year away at boarding school, even enrolling in college, were all steps Granny made her take alone. When she complained, Granny just said, "You'll be fine and you will thank me one day."

Late one December night, during Abby's first year at Emory, a massive heart attack caused Granny to slip away in her sleep. That was the first time Abby doubted Granny's words. That is when her parents' death became the second worse day of her life and she did not feel strong at all. However, with the help of her best friend and roommate, Rachel and her boyfriend, Abby made it through the grieving process.

Now, Tom and Rachel smiled down from their wedding picture on the bookshelf, reminding Abby of her close bond with those two. They were the nearest thing to family she had on this earth and, she reminded herself, they were the reason she met James. She bubble-wrapped the picture and placed it in the nearest open box, a seemingly symbolic move to dissipate her doubts of making this move.

With a surge of energy, Abby plowed through the purge and pare process with newfound excitement. Thinking of James and her friends helped changed her mood and outlook, but Abby knew Granny's words of strength were her real impetus.

The next few days passed quickly and when the movers drove away, Abby stood in the empty apartment, proclaiming a silent goodbye to her past to make room for her new life in North Carolina. Her last task as a Georgia native would be to drop off the key to the property owner and fill her tank with gas for the trip.

As she drove off, Abby shed no tears. She had cried them all out the day before when she said goodbye to her co-workers. These agents had been her life since she left Quantico. Not only had they worked together, they often, spent long and dangerous hours watching each other's backs. She had genuine respect for these people and had gained a wealth of investigative skills during the past eighteen months, knowledge she would take with her to the Raleigh Field Office. She was indeed fortunate to have learned from the best.

Six hours and three phone calls to James later, Abby drove up to the parsonage. She saw him, sitting in the porch swing, waving with a big grin splashed across his face. His boyish leapfrog over the porch railing and shrubs to greet her, made her shake her head. He was, she had found, a child at heart.

"Welcome home." James' words melted into a kiss. Finally, breaking apart to add, "I've missed you something crazy."

About that time, Tom came out to greet her, explaining that Rachel would soon be home from the hospital.

"I just appreciate having a place to stay for now."

"You know our house is your house as long as you need it. Plus, you're real close to the war room." Tom gave her a wink.

Abby would stay at the parsonage and her furniture would remain in storage until she found a place to rent. With her job in Raleigh starting in just two weeks, she needed to find somewhere soon. As much as she would like, she hoped Tom did not expect her to spend all her free time in the war room. After all, now there was James and he needed her time.

She no longer felt pressure to solve this case in days or weeks, like when she was just visiting. That meant it would be easy to become complacent. Not only would she be here full time now, the help of local law enforcement — well, one, at least should make the job a little easier...

After a late afternoon drive with James to look for rental property and, of course, a trip to Clark Lake, they met Rachel and Tom back at the church.

"Find anything interesting?" Rachel asked, shaking her head and giving the two a knowing look. "For rent, I mean. You were gone a long time."

Thinking back on their last minute stop by the lake, Abby realized she still must have that certain glow.

"Actually, we did see one particularly nice place." Abby shot James a look. Did he catch her little joke? His subtle cough confirmed that he did.

"Look, guys, it's nearly 9:30. I'm sure Abby is tired after

driving all day." Tom sounded impatient. "Why don't we have a quick look at the war room so we can all get to bed? We can talk about her house hunt tomorrow."

Good old Tom.

When he flipped the wall switch in the basement, light flooded across the rogues gallery of persons of interest, Abby caught herself letting out a little gasp. It had only been a few weeks since she had been in the room but the amount of information that filled this space was impressive, even to her. All the faces on display had been just sitting there, awaiting her return.

"Are you guys up for a quick review of what we have so far?" Suddenly, time meant nothing to a re-energized Abby. They pulled up chairs; four unlikely sleuths, meeting in an unlikely place, at an unlikely time, to solve what was, most likely, an unsolvable crime. Crazy? Probably, but Abby had never felt so alive.

"Let's start with my visit with the Senator. I think we can safely presume that Ashton fathered Jessie's baby and the good Senator arranged and financed a private adoption. Most likely, he paid Theo to keep quiet, too."

Noting the skepticism on Tom's face, Abby added, "Theo Cline, a loose cannon most of the time, was leverage for Connors'. His campaign was at stake."

"Okay," Tom nodded. "So, that gives Connors a motive?"

"Could be we're headed in the right direction, at least. But, if we look at these pictures, just about all of them had some sort of motive to see her dead." Abby walked up to the boards and picked up a black marker. "Let's just mark off all those without a motive."

148

She looked to her friends then pointed to Tom. "Talk to me."

"Well, we certainly can't rule out the Connors, either one of them. Especially after your visit to the Senator's office."

Abby moved to the next picture: Ashton Connors' mug shot from the day of the murder. There were, in fact, three different shots of Ashton holding up his identification plate in each quarter-turn pose. In the straight-on shot, bulging, glassy eyes stared into the camera lens. They were the only parts of his face not covered with either dirt or hair. His curly locks were matted and hung in clumps.

"This must have been mug shot number seven or eight." James chimed in. "Don't know why they even bother anymore. Guess these the only pictures there are of him since he was a child."

James then shared the only other bit of information about Ashton gleaned from the official records of the murder.

"If you look close, you'll notice that the date he was picked up was October 30, 1998 but he was not actually booked until the next day. That's because our department was engrossed in Jessica Cline's murder. No one had time to do paperwork on the town drunk until later. At least, that gave Ashton plenty of time to sleep it off."

James shook his head and added, "They said Ashton's only reaction when he came out of his fog that morning was to look down at his latest cell tag and ask why he was there. The report said the jailer just shook her head and answered, 'the usual'. Ashton said, "Damn, you act like I committed murder or something."

That statement may have sounded alarms if he had not

already been behind bars when the crime took place.

"And, for that reason alone, Ashton can be crossed off the list of suspects." Abby pulled the cap from the marker and drew a big "X" through Ashton's name and picture'

She moved over to the next board containing Wesley and Nolan's mug shot and turned to James. "Deputy?"

"The Cline brothers cannot be ruled out simply because they're kin. Those two are bad guys, for sure; mean drunks who were, no doubt, abusive to their sister. Theo is mean, too. Could they get mad enough, drunk enough, to kill another family member?" James shook his head. "Wow, I hope not."

Abby moved on down the lineup.

"Then, there's bootlegger, Pop Melvin and his goon-of-a-son, Tuke. Jessie was a frequent customer of theirs." Abby turned to Rachel for this one.

"They had a motive. She, probably, owed Pop a lot of money... or, maybe she threatened to turn him in to the authorities."

James interrupted her. "Rachel! All this time I thought you were a true southerner. Don't tell me you don't know this scenario."

He chuckled as he continued. "For years, the law here in Rose County has allowed Pop to run his liquor business, ignoring every illegal move he made. I asked about it once. Omar never came right out and told me, but he eluded to a 'gentleman's agreement', struck years before, between former Sheriff Buck Stevens and Pop. The county would leave him alone if Pop gave up a few patrons along the way. So, for years, anyone with an unpaid tab, might just be arrested for drunk driving shortly after leaving Pop's. It was a plan that worked well. Pop's business flourished, as did the arrest quota for the department. Pop's patrons either paid up, sobered up, or got locked up"

James noticed the disapproving stare from Rachel and Tom.

"Don't tell me ya'll don't have the same thing going on down there in Georgia." James knew he was right. "Anyway, all that changed when illegal drugs, not just moonshine, came on the scene. While I don't think Jessie would be killed for snitching on Pop over liquor, drugs may be a whole new game."

"It's a long shot, but let's keep them on our 'motive' list." Abby had only taken the cap off the marker for one of the suspects so far.

There was no picture for the last person of interest, just a silhouette of the nameless stranger who passed through town and killed Jessica Cline. As reported, this man had picked up Jessie as she walked, alone, along the highway in the wee hours of October 31, 1998. Possible, But why? The motive was all speculation.

"I pulled our crime scene report, just to make sure it matched what you had." James pulled out the folder from the box he had brought in the day before. He shuffled through to the conclusions page.

"And everything lines up. The official report states: a stranger, traveling down Highway 37, possibly a soldier traveling from Camp Lejeune to Fort Bragg, sees Jessica walking down the road. He stops and offers her a ride."

"Wait," Abby interrupts. "James, as you read, will you explain the investigative principles ya'll used to draw your conclusions in this situation?"

"Sure." James continued. "The reason to suspect a soldier?

Because Highway 37 provides a straight shot through the hundred-mile stretch of road connecting the two military bases. The soldiers often make that drive between midnight and five in the morning when there is less traffic."

After looking for his friends to acknowledge that they understood, James read more from the report.

"They didn't drive far before he turned onto Old Post Road and pulled his car up behind an abandoned tobacco barn." James added, "Remember, Old Post Road is barely a mile from the Cline farm.

"They drank and had sex, and then each smoked a cigarette before the attack. He forced her to partially disrobe before chasing her through a corn field with a knife." James put down the report to explain that investigators found two empty beer cans and two cigarette butts behind the barn, near fresh tire tracks. They found Jessica's underpants and one shoe there, as well. The absence of her blood on those items indicated she tried to run before he stabbed her.

"Possibly, she saw what he intended to do and knew she had to try to get away. Investigators followed a trail of scattered and ripped clothing, indicating the killer tore the garments from the fleeing victim as she ran. The trail became a bloody path that zigzagged through the cornfield. It stopped with a pool of blood at the point where she finally fell, at the opposite end of Old Post Road."

"He managed to inflict thirty-seven stab wounds before she collapsed. Most were defensive blows – meaning he drew the knife in a downward motion as she tried to get away. She fought to the end until her attacker cut her throat with such force she was near decapitation. The perpetrator's bloodstained footprints led back to his car and tire tracks indicate that he sped away in the direction of Fort Bragg. Jessica bled out quickly and was left for the newspaper guy to find on the side of the road."

Tom and Rachel looked stunned, as though they had been eyewitnesses to the awful Halloween killing.

"Wow." That was all Tom could say.

"Sounds to me like it could really have happened that way." Rachel looked at Abby. "Makes sense to me."

"Well it doesn't make sense to me." Abby jumped up to the board, ready to state her case. She grabbed a marker and drew a circle around the faceless suspect.

"Think about it, guys. The serial killer scenario is too convenient—a lazy way to solve a crime. Possible? Yes. However, I just don't buy it. Surely, someone at a gas station or truck stop between Eden Falls and Fort Bragg would notice a stranger, covered in blood. And if he got to Bragg without stopping, the MP's would have noticed him at a check point." Abby sat back down.

"She's right", James added. "The person who committed this crime would have a hard time not being noticed, even on Halloween. Besides, how would a stranger know where park, out of sight, on Old Post Road? Moreover, serial killers usually feel the need to repeat their crime using similar methods. We tracked this for weeks; no murders similar to this were reported anywhere in North Carolina."

Throwing up his hands, James added, "Seems this serial killer just struck one time then vanished into thin air."

"Which is why I say, a stranger didn't kill Jessica Cline." Abby chimed back in. "Most transient serial killers don't commit crimes this way. They strike and flee, then move on to the next victim. They certainly do not take time to chase their prey through an unfamiliar cornfield. And robbery couldn't have been the motive since her purse, identification, and thirty dollars remained at the scene."

Rachel chimed in. "If someone had solicited her as a prostitute, they were probably just after sex, not blood — and if she had tried to rip him off, making him mad enough to kill, why would he leave money and so much evidence behind?" She seemed to be reading Abby's mind

"Exactly." Abby glanced at her watch. "The biggest reason I don't think a stranger did it is because of all those stab wounds — 37, 38? Then near-decapitation? A murder? No, this was overkill. Shows me it was a crime of passion, and strangers don't commit that kind of crime."

"So do we agree that we can rule this one out?" Everyone nodded. Abby picked up the marker again and drew a big black "X" over the nameless silhouette on the board.

James walked over to the box of evidence he had slipped out of his makeshift office storage room. He pulled out a large paper bag and, proudly, held it up.

"I found something that may help us out." James stood there and grinned.

"Is that what I hope it is?" Abby motioned for James to open the bag.

The bag was stamped EVIDENCE. Inside were three, gallon-size Ziploc bags. One held two beer cans. One bag contained two, cigarette butts, and the other bag was labeled, "victim's panties". Abby was sure it contained Jessica's DNA. All they had to do was find the owner of the other DNA and they would have her killer.

She glanced at her watch again. Three o'clock. She had been up nearly twenty-four hours. She had driven nearly six hundred miles to her new home, re-acquainted herself with the war room, and finally got what could be a viable break in the murder case. All that, plus welcome home sex with James.

Overall, it had been a good day.

13.

June 15, 1999
James Wilcox

"There's absolutely no reason for you to pay those Raleigh prices for rent when you can stay here for free."

James practiced that line all the way to pick up Abby for her bi-weekly home search. He had offered for her to stay at the lake house several times before but, each time, her answer was a firm, "No". However, there were few homes for rent around Eden Falls and those that they found were miles out of town in the opposite direction. Clark Lake was half way between Eden Falls and Raleigh, an easy commute so, this time he hoped she would agree.

Much to his surprise, Abby spoke up first. "Look, James, I've made a decision. I'm tired of being homeless." She did not look at him but talked while she buckled her seat belt.

"If we don't find a place today, I will accept your offer to move into the Lake house— on one condition. I will pay rent and utilities like I would anywhere else."

Her answer thrilled James but he was a little taken aback by her demeanor. His response was simply, "Okay."

"And-" Abby bit the side of her lip, hesitating. "And, you

can't stay there with me. You cannot even spend the night. Not yet."

He looked confused and a little hurt. "Okay," he replied.

When they stopped to get coffee, she dropped a quarter in the newspaper box. It was Wednesday and Abby knew the expanded, real estate edition of the *News Tribune* would be on the shelves. She could still smell the ink as she pulled it out of the rack. Ignoring the now-stale news headlines, Abby turned to *Rental & Real Estate* section, browsing for new listings.

"Oh my God!—Look." She shoved the paper over for James to see. "Isn't this near the Cline farm?"

James tossed his coffee cup into the trash and backed the car out of the Stop & Go. "Well, let's just see."

"Nice, 2BR, 1B, for rent. $750/month, 1549 Cline Rd. Contact: Theo Cline at 910-304-6661." Abby read the ad as James drove. He pulled over when they reached the entrance to Cline Road.

"What are we going to say if we run into Theo?" Abby was getting excited about having a reason to make contact with Theo. Still, she did not want to spook him or make him mad for not calling first.

"We'll just tell him the truth. You're looking for a house to rent." James quickly added. "But, I don't care if it's the Tahj Mahal, if I have my say, you will never live on Cline Road."

"Why Deputy, that sounds like a challenge." Abby quipped but thought to herself, *you got that one right!*

The car slowly crept around the curves of Cline Road with both passengers straining to see the rental house.

"Must be past the home place. I never saw any other

house down here. In fact, I do not think I have even been past the big house. Never had a reason to." James slowed as he approached Theo's big rundown mansion, half-expecting to see him on the porch. No one was in sight. Only when they were well past the yard and hidden by the trees, were Abby and James relieved enough to take a tandem deep breath. Then, no more than twenty yards away, a little house came into view.

"Well, imagine that!" James laughed. Only someone as strange as Theo Cline could think of trying to rent out this dwelling, he thought. "Let's take a look."

They walked around the wooden structure that looked to have been a small tenant house, about thirty years old. Weeds had grown up around the front steps that led to the rotten boards of the front porch. Trying to look inside was futile through windows caked with dirt. A broken padlock hung from the doorframe so entry would not have been a problem—if someone wanted to go inside. Obviously, it appeared no one had lived here for a long time.

"This place gives me the creeps." James agreed with Abby. "Let's get out of here!"

Leaving the cover of the trees, James pulled the car back onto the narrow road and back past the Cline home.

"Aghhhhh!" They both screamed when James slammed on brakes, just in time to keep from hitting Theo. He stood there, legs spread wide and planted firmly in the middle of the road, his shotgun aimed towards their windshield. James and Abby raised their hands in the air in surrender.

Theo slowly turned the gun away and walked towards the car. James rolled down the window.

"Good Lord, James. I thought you was a prowler." Theo turned his head and spat on the ground. "What the hell you doin' here?"

James gave him the story about looking for a house to rent and Abby held the newspaper up for him to see.

"About time they got that in the paper—should've been in there last week. Idiots! Ya'll want to see it?" Theo pointed back towards the path.

"No thanks, Theo. We saw it already...don't think she's interested. A little too much work to do."

"Aw, are you talkin' 'bout that first little house up here?" Theo pointed to the run down dwelling they just left. "That ain't it! The rental's about a quarter mile down there. Just wait, I'll get the key." Theo turned to go back towards the house when James stopped him.

"Wait, Theo. We are sorry. We should have called first. We'll come back later." James was easing his foot off the brake pedal as he spoke. Abby waved.

"I didn't mean to scare you." Theo shouted as they pulled away. "Just shows what a good landlord I'd be. I can protect whoever lives down there. Won't let nothing happen to 'em."

"We will call you!" James floored it.

After a good laugh, they both realized they had stumbled onto an excellent opportunity. Abby's house hunt was the perfect ruse for an undercover interrogation of the Clines. Theo did not need to know that she had no intention of him ever being her landlord.

They headed to Clark Lake. Abby's house hunt was over.

James and Abby were still laughing and talking about their adventure on Cline Road when they pulled back up to the parsonage. Since they were back early, they knew Rachel would not be home from work yet. Still, this news was too good to wait. They just had to share it with Tom and headed straight for the war room. Tom was not there.

"What's wrong with us? It's Wednesday." Abby tapped her forehead remembering. "Tom's in his office. He always starts his sermon on Wednesday. Let's go to the house and find a cold drink. We can wait for him to take a break"

They tiptoed into the kitchen so as not to disturb the working pastor. Abby pulled two Cokes from the fridge and popped open the cans and led James out to the front porch glider.

"Now," she said, "what are we going to say to Theo when we go to see his 'rental property'?"

"Well, whatever we say, it has to get us into the main house. I haven't been inside, nor seen Myra for that matter, since right after the murder." James knew they had to make the best of this opportunity. "I'll call Theo tomorrow—"

James turned towards the open screen door. "Did you hear that?"

"No," Abby said. "Wait, yes I do." She chuckled. "That's just Tom practicing his sermon."

"Wow, guess I didn't realize he practiced out loud."

James continued, "Okay, back to the Clines. I'll call Theo tomorrow..." Again, he stopped in mid-sentence and turned to Abby. "Are you sure Tom's okay in there? He's very loud. I've never heard him shout during a service—not even a fiery one. He's not that kind of preacher."

"Think we should check on him?" Abby pulled James up and motioned for him to follow her back inside, holding her finger against her lips in a shush sign.

As they tiptoed down the hallway, Tom's voice got louder but try as they may, neither James nor Abby could make out his words. It was as though he was speaking a foreign language.

"What the hell is that?" James whispered.

"Shush!" Abby turned to walk away, pulling James by the arm. "I don't know but let's not let him catch us standing here like were spying on him."

Turning to leave, James stepped on a squeaky floorboard and Abby bumped against the wall. Both froze in place and, at the same moment, Tom's foreign-sounding words stopped.

When the office door opened, Abby was already apologizing for interrupting Tom's work. James started to explain, as well, but he could see that Tom was clearly embarrassed at being caught practicing aloud. Neither friend asked about the strange language they heard.

"Oh, that's alright." Tom seemed out of breath. "Guess I was just caught up in the moment in there. Getting ready for Sunday, you know." Sweat poured from his brow as he thanked them for the interruption. It was time for a break, anyway. "Besides, Rachel should be home soon."

James followed Tom into the kitchen and Abby pulled another Coke from the refrigerator.

"What have you two done today? Any progress on the house hunt?"

James and Abby filled Tom in on the Theo Cline story. They were discussing their plan to revisit the Clines, when Rachel walked in from work. With the team together, they discussed details of how to take full advantage of the situation.

James even made a call to Theo from the parsonage.

"He said for Abby and I to meet him at eleven in the morning." James turned to Abby and added, "You know what that means—"

"We get there at ten thirty." They spoke in tandem.

"Want to catch him off guard, if possible." James said. "Don't want him to have time to prepare ahead of time. So we will get their early."

"I'm a little nervous." Rachel had been surprised to come home to this.

"I'm a little excited." Abby hugged her friend.

"Well, I don't know what kind of house they have for sale but, as your best friend, I forbid you to rent anything from Theo Cline!"

Abby looked to James. "Should we tell them?"

James nodded. "Abby won't need your hospitality any longer." He grabbed Abby's hand and kissed it gently. "She found a place to live."

Abby confessed her decision to rent the lake house from James. Rachel seemed thrilled. Tom was not.

Before they had time to review last minute plans, James' car rounded the last curve to the Cline house and into the drive where, to their surprise, Theo sat waiting for them in the front porch swing. His squinted and scowled at the arriving car as though James and Abby were trespassers instead of invitees. So much for trying to arrive early to catch him off guard.

"Just go with the plan." James told Abby as he threw up

his hand in a wave.

"Morning, Mr. Cline. Hope we're not too early for you. I know we said eleven o'clock but..."

With a quick handshake, Theo interrupted James in mid-sentence. "Better early than late," Theo said and turned away. "Follow me." Theo was walking towards his truck.

"Well, I guess we will follow him." James shrugged.

"Guess so. We can't risk raising suspicion now." Abby was disappointed at not getting inside the Cline's home.

"Well, just play along for now. Remember our story. We are an engaged couple, looking for a rental unit in a quiet area. We only have to make it last as long as we need access to the Clines." James glanced at Abby and smiled. "Hey, don't tell me we can't give a convincing performance of two people in love."

Abby leaned over, circled her arm around his waist and kissed him on the neck.

"Hey, don't make me have to pull off of this one lane road. Especially, since we're following Theo Cline." They both laughed.

Abby felt safe with this man. Somehow, she knew that James Wilcox was her true love, her protector, her very own "twofer".

As they followed Theo another half mile or so, he finally turned into the drive of a surprisingly nice three-bedroom brick ranch. "We'll be fine. For now, just play the role." James reassured her.

Abby was not nervous in the least. After all, she was a trained FBI agent. Besides, James was with her and she could see the entrance to Cline Road and Highway 37 from the back yard of the little brick house. It seems they had merely circled the entire Cline farm.

"Well, this is it." Theo threw up his hand and motioned them towards the front door. "Go on in. It ain't locked."

"You first, Mr. Cline." James tried to sound as though he were simply being respectful to his elders instead of making sure Theo was not between himself and the door.

"Sure 'nough. As you see, this is a standard little ranch—two beds, one bath." Theo had suddenly taken on the role of realtor. "New carpet, new paint," was an amenity that need-ed no mention. The strong odor of paint made it smell as though the painters had just cleaned their brushes and the carpet still held fresh lines from the vacuum cleaner propped in the corner. Theo followed their every step.

"What about A/C?" James saw no sign of central air and hoped this would be their excuse for a deal breaker.

"Got two new window units coming next week. That should be plenty of air for this little place—might even be so cold it'll run you out of here." Theo chuckled then changed the subject.

"Plenty of good well water, too. Septic tank is in the side yard so make sure you don't drive your cars over there. Don't want a caved-in septic tank—you'd be surprised how often that happens in the sandy soil around here."

James held up his hand to stop Theo from thinking they had made the decision to take the place. "Thanks Mr. Cline. I think Abby and I have seen enough. The place is very nice—you've done a great job with it. But I hate for you to stand out here in this heat. Why don't Abby and I talk this over and get back to you." James was guiding Abby out the door.

"Oh no you don't!" Theo's command stops the couple in their tracks.

"You just stop up at the house for a minute. —Get a cool drink and meet Myra. Even if you don't rent the place, I can't send you away hot and thirsty." Theo scooted past James and out the door. "Just leave the door open. Need to get that paint smell out, anyway."

Once in the car, Abby and James agreed to keep their eyes and ears open while they make nice with the Cline family.

"So, what brought you to Eden Falls, Miss Rials?" Myra Cline held out the tray for Abby and James to take their glasses of iced tea before setting it on the small wicker table between the ornate wicker chairs and loveseat that decorated the massive front porch. Abby was disappointed that Myra offered them a seat on the porch. She had wanted to see inside the massive house partly from an investigators standpoint but also, because she loved old things and was certain the Cline house held many antiques. Still, there was lots to see on the porch. The wicker furniture, all twelve pieces, held the same ornate embellishments and were worn, missing white paint in matching areas, proof that this furniture had sat in the same spot for many years. Abby recognized the glasses Myra served tea from were vintage crystal and the silver tray was heavy sterling. They probably used priceless antiques every day, not due to pretentiousness but because they always had. This impressed Abby more than anything.

"I came to visit my best friend from college, Rachel Kirby. You might know her husband, Tom Kirby; he's the preacher at Bethel Baptist Church." Abby took a sip of the sweet beverage and waited for a response.

165

"Of course I know the Kirby's—nice people. Cute couple, too." Myra seemed content to entertain on the front porch. "You and James make a cute couple, too. Theo told me you two are engaged. Why that's just wonderful. Let me see the ring." Myra reached for Abby left hand and found a naked ring finger.

"Ah, I don't have it yet." Myra had taken Abby by surprise. "I mean—"

Myra stopped Abby. "Lord, I'm sorry for that. I didn't mean to be so nosey. It's just that I get excited for young people in love, especially when I know them." Then, turning to James, she added, "I remember James when he was just a little boy. Hard to believe he's grown up enough to be getting' married."

James spoke up. "That's okay, Miss Myra. Abby's ring is still at the jewelry store. It was too big, so they're sizing it for her." James glanced at Abby who still looked flustered. "Why don't we stop by next week and show it to you?"

"Yes, I'd love to see it. Don't make a special trip but if you-re out this way—"Myra grinned. I so seldom have company and I don't drive. It gets kind of lonesome living out here with no body to talk to, you know."

"Myra!"Theo's loud voice preceded the slam of the screen door. "Leave James and Miss Rials alone. They're probably gonna' rent the little house so you'll see them all the time. But don't run 'em off before they decide."

"That's okay, Mr. Cline." James intervened. "You are bound to be ready for a cold glass of tea. I know you've been working hard this morning." He then backed Theo into a porch rocker and slapped a glass of tea in his hand before

Theo knew what had happened.

Abby, impressed at how James handled the old man, took the opportunity to begin a gracious exit.

"Thank you, so much for the tea, Mrs. Cline." Abby held out a hand to their host who clasped it with both of hers. Myra had a look of disappointment that made Abby feel a little guilty to leave so abruptly.

James thanked the couple and thanked them for the tour of the rental house.

"When you gonna' get back with me?" Theo shouted from his rocker.

As he closed the passenger door, James turned and, as though in afterthought and shouted towards the Clines. "It may be the end of next week, Mr. Cline. I have to be in Charlotte until Wednesday for a conference. But I'll contact you as soon as I get back."

"The place won't stay empty long, you know." Theo managed to sit up straight in his porch rocker although not committed to actually standing to wave goodbye. Then, he leaned back and started the rhythmic squeak of the chair. Theo's workday appeared to be over.

"What was that? You're going out of town?" Abby said as they drove away from the Cline home. She hoped James had made up the Charlotte trip just to buy some time from having to contact Theo.

"Yeah—sorry, I forgot to tell you. It's a Sheriff's Conference, an annual thing, something to help us get continuing education credits. It's only three days—say you're welcome to go with me if you want."

Abby laughed. "As much fun as I can imagine a Sheriff's Conference to be, no thank you. I just hope you realize that I do not like that kind of surprise. Besides," Abby giggled and slipped back into their role-playing. "We're supposed to be engaged, you know. You're supposed to share that kind of thing with you fiancé." Abby feigned disappointment.

James winced. "Oh, yeah—sorry. That reminds me." He winked. "We need to pick up that engagement ring. Want you to be able to show it to Ms. Cline when we come back." Then he grinned and brushed her cheek with a soft touch. Abby thought she saw a serious look in his eyes and her heart skipped a beat.

Tom searched around for another thumbtack and an empty space to insert a newfound picture of Theo. The team stared at the most recent photo of the elder Cline found in a church directory in 1992, tagged with his full name, Richard Theodore Cline. Theo, wearing an out-of-style suit and tie, looked uncomfortable in front of the camera. His white shirt, most likely purchased just for this occasion, enhanced the odd color and leathery appearance of his skin. A combination of farmer's tan and alcohol-induced jaundice were noticeable contrasts to the bright white of his shirt and the shock of white hair against his leathery forehead. Sitting, stone-faced, beside Myra, he looked much older than age sixty. Tom thought he could see a twinge of pain in Theo's eyes. Arthritis, perhaps?

Something about the old man in the picture reminded Tom of his own father, the senior Reverend Kirby. He was never comfortable in front of the camera, either. He suffered from arthritis and made alcohol his anesthetic of choice. Tom wondered if Myra had nagged Theo into posing for this picture. That is what his mother would have done. She would have begged him to stay sober just long enough to get through the photo session.

For years, the elder Kirby hid his alcoholism from the congregation but he never fooled his family and his wife became his enabler. Tom's mother protected her husband and covered for him when necessary. She was in denial, satisfied with keeping him sober a few hours at a time. Denial was an easy way for her to postpone a crisis. He thought he could see that same trait in Theo's wife. Tom's mother and Myra Cline could be soul sisters pledged to the same passive-aggressive sorority.

"To me, Theo Cline is a troubling character." James was the first to speak up, pacing as he talked. "Something makes me think he did it – or knows who did, and I'm not basing that on his looks. This man," James points to the photograph, "is capable of killing. I know it in my gut. But gut feelings don't hold up well in court."

Abby pulled up a clean bulletin board. "Well, we don't have to act like we're in a courtroom just yet. I have an idea."

Transferring Theo's picture to the new board, she gave it a label: GUT FEELING SUSPECTS.

"Next?" Abby looked to the others.

"Let's talk about this guy." Rachel pointed to the mug shot of another suspect, cleared during the initial investigation. She tacked up his picture.

"George (Pop) Melvin – Rose County's best known

bootlegger. Can you add something, James, personally or professionally?"

"Sure." James smiled when he saw Pop's picture. "Personally, I can tell you that anyone who grew up here either knows or has heard of him. As you see from this picture, he looks like any ordinary seventy-five year old black man from these parts and that's what he wants people to think. Quick to tell folks he is just a poor old retired farmer who spends his days fishing in Beaver Dam or whittling wooden toys for his grandchildren, the gray-haired senior citizen sure looks harmless. He's friendly and outgoing and loves to flash his gold tooth every time he grins."

Professionally speaking, James said that authorities considered Pop little more than a nuisance. For years, local law enforcement looked other way when it came to the sideline business he ran out of his barn. Rather than arrest an old man for selling homemade liquor, they preferred to arrest his customers, the true criminals.

For years, Pop would randomly signal a nearby cruiser that a drunk driver was on Highway 37 and 'Voila!' One less dangerous drunk driver on the road. Of course, no one explained that Pop had served said liquor to the drunk driver who, coincidentally, probably owed Pop a sizeable unpaid tab.

"Omar liked that arrangement." James shook his head. "After a while, no matter our personal feelings about the practice – well, it had just gone on for too long."

Abby jumped in. "The local version of prohibition-era protection. I get it. Tom, were you able to talk to anyone near Pop's?"

"Sure did. I presented myself as the new pastor and spoke

with several of Pop's neighbors.

Everyone loves him." Tom said. "And everyone knows about what James said. They view it as victimless crime and consider the authorities' practice of turning a blind eye too difficult to change.

"One neighbor told me, 'Trying to stop that now would be like grabbing a wolf by the ears. You know you should have never done it but you're too damned scared of what will happen when you let go.' Then he added, 'Pardon my cuss, Preacher.'

"I did learn that Theo and sons had been good customers for Pop over the years and before her death, Jessica had joined them as regulars. Pop usually bartered with the Clines, seldom exchanging cash for liquor, but if their tab ever got out of hand, Pop just sent Tuke to collect."

Tom went on to explain that Tuke Melvin, Pop's son, was a one-man collection agency. He weighed over 350-pounds and had to do little more than show up to elicit a payment from past due customers.

"When I left Pop's, I went to the Cline farm — asked Myra if she knew Tuke. She said yes. He had been to the house a couple of times looking for Theo. He was always polite, she said, never threatening. He never said why he was there and she did not ask. Did not have to – Myra knew Theo owed money to the bootlegger."

"One question," Rachel chimed in. "Were the Melvin's ever officially questioned about Jessica's murder?"

James pulled out more notes. "Sure were. On November 2, 1998, deputies picked up Pop and Tuke for an informal interview. The two expressed appropriate shock and sadness at hearing of Jessica's murder. Pop admitted she came by his establishment now and then for beer and cigarettes. Tuke said Pop, most times, just wrote off her purchases. That was because he thought so much of that cute little Cline girl.

The notes included a statement by Pop. "I swear, Sheriff, if anyone gets up a posse to search for her killer, you can count on me and my son to help." Then, Tuke added. "And you know my Pa don't lie." There was a handwritten note in the margin of the report. It read— *When Tuke spoke, Pop flashed a gold-toothed grin.*

"Entertainment factor aside," James continued, "On November 10, 1998, ALE and ATF agents carried out a late night raid at Pop's store. They did not find illegal drugs, alcohol, or any evidence that would tie them to the murder. They did find, however, several unpaid tabs for Jessica Cline and Ashton Connors. Twelve charge tickets spanning nine days. Twelve sixteen-ounce, beers at twenty-five dollars each – three hundred dollars remained unpaid.

"Price gouging? Yes. A motive for murder? Most likely. Not."

The team took a vote. Neither Pop nor Tuke remained viable suspects, not even as gut feeling suspects.

After a quick bathroom break, the four pulled up their chairs for the last hour of work. Before taking her seat, Rachel walked around the room, looking at the boxes and stacks of papers that seemed to be growing.

"Look at the slobs we have become."

For months, paper had been coming in but none was going out. Rachel pointed to the fancy crosscut shredder. Purchased before Abby's arrival, it was still in the box.

"Yeah, I was noticing that, too." James looked around at the ever-growing piles of paper. "When you guys started this project, how did you plan to explain this to anyone who might, even accidentally, discover your war room?"

The room went silent. It was as though the thought never occurred to any of them. Tom crossed his arms as though he was ready for the debate.

"What do you mean when you call it 'our' war room? I thought you were one of us now – a part of the team. Are you making fun of what we're doing here? Maybe Rachel and I do not have any professional police training but you said yourself that we've done a good job, thus far. So—"

"What? – No!" James was surprised at Tom's reaction.

Rachel stepped up. "Tom, you know James didn't mean anything like that."

Tom was not convinced. He seemed to be getting more and more agitated pacing back and forth, stopping in front of James. "Just remember, you, Deputy, are one of us now. So, if anyone does find this place, you are just as involved as us."

James held up both hands to Tom.

"Look, you guys named it the war room before I ever saw this place. That is what I meant by calling it yours. Heaven knows I would do anything to help solve this case and protect my community." Now James' temper was showing. "After all, wasn't I the one who came out here a few months ago to warn you about recent break-ins in nearby churches?"

"Stop it!" Abby stood beside James and shot her eyes at the preacher. "James brings up a good point. We need to start purging some of these notes and files we don't need, especially all the stuff we have scanned into the computer.

All this would be hard to explain if accidentally found. We would all look like devil-worshipers and Tom — you would be fired for sure."

"Tell you what." Abby sat down and lowered her voice. "I'll spend the next few days shredding the scanned documents. James will be in Charlotte until Wednesday and my job does not start for another week. Other than moving in a few boxes at the lake house, I have nothing better to do. Agreed?"

Everyone nodded. They all looked tired. Tom looked tired and tentative.

❄

"Well, that was a quick move." James placed three suitcases on the floor next to the six boxes sealed with packing tape. They had managed to get everything in their cars making it a one-trip move from the parsonage to the cabin.

"I'm ready for a break, how about you?" James fell onto the couch and stretched open his arms.

A pillow to his face was Abby's reply.

She dragged the largest suitcase into the bedroom, opening it on the floor and began to pull out pieces of clothing. She placed each garment across the bed in preparation to organize the closet. She had learned through her travels with the Bureau, to leave her clothes on hangers when she packed, finding it saved a huge amount of time when unpacking and kept her clothes from wrinkling. Smart packing, as she liked to call it, had become one of her favorite inventions and a neat-freak's best friend.

However, when she opened the closet, she found it

174

already full. About half the space held some of James' clothing. The rest of the space held hangers. Not just hangers but flimsy, plastic store hangers and, worst of all, wire hangers. That's when Abby realized James was sorely in need of a smart packing tutorial.

Abby grabbed a handful of the substandard hangers and was about to lodge her first complaint to James about his organizational skills when she turned to see him standing at the bedroom door. A big box was in his hands and look of confusion was on his face.

"Where do you want this?"

"Isn't it labeled?" Abby asked.

"Well – yes – sort of." He twisted his neck to read the side label. "I'm not sure I know where LIFE STUFF goes. I could have chosen to bring in another box, but they're all marked LIFE STUFF!" He stood, waiting for directions. "Just what the hell is LIFE STUFF? And where the hell does it go?"

"Well, it sure as hell doesn't go in the bedroom."

James was not through. "And why do you label boxes on the side where no one can read them instead of the top, like normal folks?"

"Because normal folks have enough sense to know that stacked boxes can't be read from the top – unless you're reading the top box!" Abby caught herself yelling for no apparent reason and she expected him to yell back. Instead, she watched him return the box to the floor in the den and flop down on the couch.

Abby tossed the hangers onto the bed and followed him. "I'm sorry I'm being such a bitch."

"I'm sorry you're being such a bitch, too." He laughed and

kissed her.

She would explain her smart packing system later and then she would remind him that all her furniture and day-to-day items were in storage, boxed and labeled "kitchen, bedroom, den," etc. She would tell him that the boxes labeled LIFE STUFF were just for comfort, the ones she always kept with her in temporary living situations. Wherever she was, she would always have familiar things to open and quickly make her surroundings feel like home. Some of Granny's dishes and towels, even an old welcome mat from the house where she grew up, gave her a sense of place and belonging. A LIFE STUFF box is just that — life stuff and, as to where it belongs, she will not know until it is open and the memories fall out.

James would hear all that later but for now, that was not her priority. Abby pulled him from the couch. He protested until she led him back into the bedroom where she pushed all the clothes and hangers onto the floor. Their hands moved quickly to undress each other, adding jeans, tee shirts and underwear to the pile of clothes on the floor.

Abby had to remind herself — priorities change.

The girls were engrossed in planning a fun day out, involving shopping for things to decorate a lakeside cabin. They did not hear the knock on the door until it became a bang.

"Why is the door locked?" Tom looked puzzled. "I need a little help here."

"Sorry, Hon. Remember, we decided to keep the door locked all the time." Rachel held the door for Tom to drag in a large trash bin and point to another in the hallway. "Especially while we are here and this proves why." She rolled the second bin inside and locked the door behind her.

"Yep." Abby said. "If we were all in here, talking, like we usually are we may not hear a knock or someone come in without knocking."

The work inside the war room had taken on a new air of urgency. After the near meltdown on Friday, the group seemed ready to put their squabbles behind them and finish the clean-up job. As they waited for James to join them, the three talked about a renewed commitment. Knowing there would always be personality clashes to handle and work schedules to juggle, Abby, Rachel, and Tom renewed their vow to find Jessica Cline's killer. They agreed to respect each other more when it came to personal time and work schedules. Still, Abby felt an unspoken agreement to forgive but not forget hung in the air.

Tom conceded but still seemed angry. He then decided to argue about where to put the bins and who would be responsible for taking them out. After a five-minute rant from Tom about locked doors and trash bins, Abby was ready to kill Tom.

"Why stop with one murder." Abby whispered to herself.

Tom hushed when he heard a loud knock at the door.

"Glad to see you remembered to lock the door." It was James, who came in flashing a big but temporary grin. Noting the discordant look on Tom's face, he added, "What the hell is wrong now?"

14.

September 13, 1999
Abby Rials

Abby loved driving with the top down, the combination of feeling the bright sun and soothing breeze on her skin created the perfect sensation. And it felt even better at sixty-five miles per hour. That had been her main reason for choosing a convertible as her first new car purchase. Not always a practical choice, she had found, especially in winter, but on days like this when the sun was high and the humidity low, driving fast down a country road with the top down and the radio blaring was a cure for most any ailment. Since Abby had no ailments, this ride was pure fun, a celebratory victory lap of sorts. After transferring to a job in a beautiful new town, near friends she loved like family, she felt blessed. Adding to perfection, Abby was in love.

Her only disappointment this morning was not having Rachel in the passenger seat as they had planned the night before. That would have been reminiscent of old times, the days they would go for rides just to ride. When they were teens, out testing the speed limit and tempting fate, there was never a planned destination, they were just free spirits. They never worried about the consequences of which would be worse, a wreck or the wrath of the Georgia Highway Patrol. Thankfully, neither happened and the friends eventually grew into sensible adults who learned to live without testing danger at every opportunity. Still, this morning, Abby felt that old intangible thrill they used to share. Abby hoped she could adequately describe this feeling when she saw Rachel later.

When she turned onto Cline Road, she caught herself wishing for company for other reasons. Rachel had planned to make this impromptu visit to Myra Cline with Abby but a hospital staff meeting had come up at the last minute. Abby would make the visit alone. No problem, really, but another set of eyes and ears would be nice to have along and, of course, would have made the trip much more fun.

Myra met her at the door, flashing a welcoming smile and chortling about how nice it was to have company. She ushered Abby into the large, high-ceilinged living room. When Myra excused herself to get coffee from the kitchen, Abby noticed that the house was silent except for the ticking grandfather clock in the hallway. She offered to join Myra in the kitchen.

"Oh, no." Myra sang back from the hallway. "It's a mess in here. Besides, the boys will be in soon – they will take over the whole kitchen and will not give us a minute's peace. You just make yourself comfortable. I'll be right back."

Abby tried to relax but it was difficult in this place. Perusing her surroundings, complete with authentic Victorian furnishings and vintage wallpaper, the room made her feel as though she had stepped back in time. Just being in this museum-like space made her want to sit a little straighter and mind her manners just in case someone might be watching; not an actual person, mind you, but someone from the past, from the era of when the house was constructed.

Few people knew that Abby was a believer in the paranormal and the presence of ghosts had never frightened her. She learned, the hard way, this little quirk put some people off, so this fun fact about herself was something she seldom shared. Since losing her parents, ghosts seemed to surround and protect her. They had become synonymous with family and she drew comfort from thinking there may be spirits around to look after her, even spirits belonging to another family. She was sure Cline spirits lingered in the eaves of this old house, watching over, bringing comfort, and maybe even a little playful mischief, to its residents during the years. Sitting in this strangely calming environment, Abby realized that, at some point, she must share this unusual quirk with James. *Oh no, another confession to make.*

Myra came into the room carrying the same serving tray Abby remembered seeing her bring to the front porch, this time with coffee, sugar and cream. She still spoke of how happy she was to see Abby and told her so.

"I was hoping you would be back to see me."

Abby glanced around for Theo. She could feel his presence even when he was out of sight. The same with the Cline sons, whose brief appearance in the hallway after Myra brought in the coffee felt a little creepy. Nolan appeared semi-conscious even when trying to say hello and, though polite, Wesley's bloodshot eyes lingered a little too long over Abby's breasts when he spoke. Thankfully, during one of Nolan's mid-sentence nod-offs, Myra suggested they have Theo drive them to the store to pick up groceries. Although the brothers ignored their mother's request, at least they made their way out the front door. Obviously, this was not the first time Myra had used this excuse to get her sons to leave the room, nor did it seem to be the first time they ignored her.

"You know, I don't drive. Never learned—just too nervous, I guess. And, of course, with a house full of hungry men, my cupboards are always in need of restocking."

"Perhaps, I could give you a ride, Ms. Cline. Really, I don't mind." Abby's offer seemed to catch Myra by surprise.

"Oh, no. I could never ask you to do that." Myra glanced back towards the hallway as though expecting someone to walk into the room. "The boys don't mind going for me. But I do appreciate the offer."

"Mrs. Cline," Abby sat her cup on the tray and chose her words carefully. "I think you are a fine lady and I really like you. So, I don't want to mislead you about why I wanted to visit you today."

Myra leaned back in her chair, backing away from her visitor. Abby sensed a barrier going up.

"Please don't get me wrong. I liked you the moment we met – you actually remind me of my own mother. She was a very sweet person — like you. Which is why I have to be totally honest with you."

Initially, Abby had not planned to be so candid. Fact was, she really had no plan but, since this may be her only shot at talking to Myra Cline, she confessed her identity and true occupation. She explained her interest in Jessica's unsolved murder, told her everything except about the war room and

181

its contents. Abby shocked herself at how quickly she had confessed her motive, especially to someone who possibly was living with the enemy. Still, her confession felt right – and involuntary, as though prompted by all those Cline ancestors that inhabited the house.

"Mrs. Cline, you can be sure that my only interest in your daughter is keeping her murder investigation alive. She deserves that and you do, too. And, since I am doing this off the record, I hope you know you can confide in me if you have any concerns or feel the need to talk."

Abby sat back and awaited her host's response. Instead of words, Myra answered with tears. After a quick composure, she made clear just what her tears represented.

"You don't know how long I have waited for someone to say they had not given up hope of finding Jessie's killer. I was ready to write to the Governor — until I realized I didn't know what to ask him." Myra reached out and took Abby's hand, patting it softly with her own. "Whatever you can do, I will appreciate."

Abby gave Myra her standard disclaimer that she was not sure she would have success but she would try. She also told her, without elaborating, she thought it best if Theo not participate in their visit. Myra said nothing, just changed the subject.

"What was that?" Myra jumped from the chair and peered toward the back of the house towards what had sounded like the back door slamming shut. "Theo?" she called. There was no answer.

"I heard it, too." Abby was ready to change the subject but Myra beat her to it by asking about how the wedding plans were coming.

Add another lie to the list of those still to keep.

Before Abby could think of an adequate response, the door opened and Theo came stomping in from the kitchen.

"Well, if it's not the little book lady." He shot a near-toothless grin towards Abby who returned the greeting by glancing at Myra who gave her a little knowing nod back.

"Have you made up your mind about the house, Miz Rials?"

"That's the thing, Mr. Cline. The house is very nice but I have made other arrangements."

Theo's grin disappeared. "Oh, and what might that be?"

Myra stepped up. "Theo! That is none of your business. Can't you just thank Miss Rials for stopping by to tell us in person? Good Lord!"

Good response, Abby thought. With each interaction observed between Myra and Theo, Abby understood more of the Cline family dynamics and with that, her respect for Myra Cline grew. Myra was smart and, clearly, the most intelligent member of the family.

Abby stood to leave and thanked Myra for the coffee, reminding her that they would talk wedding plans soon. Theo grumbled a quick goodbye and retreated to the kitchen. As they walked to the door, Abby slipped her card and phone number into Myra's palm. "I'll stay in touch but call if you need me."

As she reached for the car door, a noise in the brush caught her attention. Abby looked behind her but it was nothing but a squirrel climbing a tall pine swaying in the intermittent gusty breeze. She noticed fast-moving clouds starting to form in the distance and considered putting up the top before leaving the driveway. Instead, whether motivated by confidence to beat the rain or her obscure feeling of uneasiness, Abby's need to leave the Cline property became more urgent than the pending shower. After sliding into the driver's seat, the motions of putting the key into the ignition, switching it on, and pulling the gear into reverse happened so fast they felt like one action. In her rush to leave, the tires spun out a cloud of dust.

Abby sped up planning to stop at the end of Cline Road to raise the convertible top. She was confident she could beat the clouds by taking the curves of the one-lane dirt path at an Indie 500 pace. Barely making it around the first of several downhill curves, the engine sputtered and groaned. *What was that strange noise?* She touched her foot to the brake but nothing happened. Then she pumped the brake – nothing. Abby realized the engine was dead only when turning the steering did nothing and the brakes became inoperable. The car picked up speed as she tugged at an immovable steering wheel.

Even when she remembered to switch off the engine, the car continued to take on a life of its own as perpetual motion forced the car off the path and into the dense growth along the passenger side of the vehicle. A barrier of brush and tall weeds cushioned the stop and buffered her near crash into a pine tree. When the car came to a complete stop, Abby's neck whipped her head into the doorframe.

She was out and time was a blur until fat drops of rain splashed across her cheeks and nose helping her return to consciousness. The rain had started, her convertible top was down, her car was stuck, and she had a painful lump on her head. What was worse, she was still on Cline property.

The rain stopped as quickly as it began which made the semi-conscious Abby angry at being so reckless. She sat trying to gather her thoughts, not only about what had happened but also about what to do next, when she could have sworn her car was moving again. In her confused state, Abby listened for the sound of the car's motor. All she could hear was rustling of weeds and brush. It was as though the car had sprouted legs and feet and was walking itself out of the overgrown field and back onto the path.

Maybe I'm dead. Abby quickly answered her own question. *No, my head hurts to bad for me to be dead.*

She sat there trying to make sense of what was happening. Had the ghosts from inside the Cline home followed her? Had they been her guardian angels, following her outside, down the driveway to shield her from her own carelessness. *Who knew angels were strong enough to move a car?* She relaxed at the thought.

"Hey, Miz Rials." A voice called but sounded far away.

"You okay? I don't think she hears us, Wes." This voice was closer.

"Lady!" This time, Abby recognized the voice and managed to focus her eyes enough to see the Cline brothers staring down at her from the open convertible top. She froze when Nolan, leaned in close. He smelled like liquor and when his oil-soaked hands moved towards her face, all she could see was the movement of dirt-packed yellow nails attached to calloused fingers. She was ready to scream but stopped when she realized he was just brushing the leaves

185

from her hair.

As the man lifted her from the seat, Abby heard his heavy breathing and the crunch of brush underfoot as he carried her away. She could see nothing but caught a vague whiff of what she could only describe as rotting garbage. His hand pressed her face tight against his chest, increasing the pain from her wounds with each heavy step he took. The smell of garbage, the smell of liquor, the smell of the man, all combined with searing generalized pain. Suddenly dropped onto a hard wood surface, Abby struggled to open her swollen eyes. She could not make sense of where she was but she could make out the voices of the men she heard. Nolan and Wesley were arguing but she could not understand the words.

Abby's instincts told her to stay alert but the pain, the smell, and the fear were not her only tormentors. A rat appeared in the corner, she tried to move but felt like every bone in her body was broken. When the rest of the rat family appeared, Abby let go of consciousness.

"You're going to be just fine."

Abby jumped at the voice and reached for the spot on her forehead she felt was the origin of her massive headache. A damp cloth covered the robin's egg size lump and the simple act of pulling the cloth away from her head drew her attention to a painful left shoulder and the plastic tubing taped firmly to her right arm. She opened her eyes to bright piercing light that caused her to close them again. Someone placed another cloth on her head and she squinted to see whose face eclipsed the fluorescent ceiling fixture as it moved closer. Rachel was by her side, gently, restraining her.

"Whoa, girl. Not so fast."

"Where…" Abby was confused. She hated being out of control. Her words and thoughts were discordant and this made her angry.

"Was I in a wreck? Where is my car?" She was getting agitated. "How long have I been here? Rachel? Where are you?"

Rachel had walked to the ER medication cart and returned with a syringe loaded with a mixture of pain medicine and sedatives. Her soothing voice calmed her friend while she, slowly, pushed the syringe-filled cocktail through the IV line.

"You are at Rose County Medical. Yes, you had a wreck – a little wreck, not a big one – and you are fine. You just bumped your head." Rachel could tell the meds were working. "James will be here soon."

Thanks to the Versed that now coursed through her veins, Abby heard just the first few words Rachel said and would remember none of it.

Tom and James arrived together and tore through the emergency room entrance as though they were in a race. They were both trying to talk at the same time when Rachel appeared and escorted them to the waiting area.

"Will the two of you calm down, please? She's fine."

"I want to see her." James started towards the door but Rachel stopped him. She directed both James and her husband to seats in the corner of the waiting room, away from the audience they had drawn via their dramatic hospital entrance.

She said that Myra and Theo Cline brought Abby to the Emergency Room earlier in the day. They said they did not call EMS, thinking it would be quicker to bring her by private car than wait for rescue to arrive. Abby was receiving treatment for multiple scrapes and bruises, a mild concussion, and several broken bones. They would watch her overnight and make sure she was stable before scheduling surgery to repair her fractures.

Once Rachel calmed James down and reassured him that Abby would be fine, she escorted him to Abby's bedside. Tom followed.

"She's not unconscious, just asleep. I just gave her a sedative – she should be out for a while." Rachel passed the medication keys to another nurse so she could take a break outside the hospital.

James leaned over and kissed Abby on the cheek then followed Rachel and Tom outside to the picnic area.

Coming directly from the Charlotte Convention Center to the hospital, James had not taken time to stop by the house. Hell, he was in such a hurry to get to the hospital that he made the three-hour drive in just over two. After Tom called him with the news that Abby had been in an accident, he had tossed his bag and briefcase into the backseat and left the Queen City as fast as he could. Though not one to, usually, take advantage of the benefits of being in law enforcement, today he was happy to be driving a marked car so he could speed. A leather notebook and loose handouts from the final seminar lay on the front seat.

He had stopped for coffee once before arriving at Rose County Medical Center where he met Tom in the parking lot. After making sure Abby was sleeping, safely under the care of the best emergency room supervisor, Rachel, and a quick briefing from Tom about the incident, the two men traveled the six miles to Cline Road.

As he got into the passenger side, Tom pulled the notebook and loose papers from underneath him and glanced at them before tossing them on top of the briefcase in the back.

"Sorry to call you away from the conference like that but I knew you'd want to get home as soon as possible."

"You know I appreciate it, Tom." James shook his head in confusion. "Guess I just don't know what she was thinking, driving like that on that road — why did she go there by herself anyway? I just don't get it." His voice projected frustration. "That is one stubborn woman."

"Yeah," Tom agreed. "She's been like that as long as I've known her, self-sufficient and thinks she can do it all. Guess that's why Rachel and I were not surprised when she wanted to work with the FBI. It's as if she has always had to prove she did not need anyone – that is until she met you. I thought you had softened her a little." Tom shrugged. "Guess I was wrong."

"What does that mean? I know Abby dated several guys in Atlanta." James was not anxious to discuss their relationship with Tom but saw this as an opportunity to show Tom his true intentions towards Abby. James knew Tom still did not trust him completely and might even consider him a double agent since being, abruptly, brought into the investigation.

"Oh, yeah. She had several boyfriends." Tom responded. "And every one of them ended just like this – with her taking off on a tangent and doing things her own way. I'm telling you, James, if you plan a permanent relationship with this girl, you had better be ready to put up with this kind of thing."

"Not sure I'm following you, Tom"

"Awe, come on, James. I heard you tell Abby to wait until you returned to have any more contact with the Clines. Besides, I have ridden with her. I know how fast she drives." Tom shook his head. "There's no telling what shape her car is in. I bet it's totaled."

James stopped himself from telling Tom that he trusted Abby completely, as a driver and investigator. Nor had he told to why he had asked Abby to wait for his return to revisit the Clines.

His plan had been to propose to Abby this coming Saturday night. Before leaving for Charlotte, James made reservations at The Wellington House, an exclusive restaurant in Raleigh. After dinner, he was going to get on one knee and ask her to be his wife then present her with the engagement ring now locked in the glove box. Since he never questioned her response, James had reserved a room at the Regency where they would celebrate by making love, making plans, and anticipating a perfect future together. Finally, after telling their family and friends, they would visit Myra Cline to show her Abby's "re-sized" diamond ring.

"How quickly plans change." James muttered to himself.

"What?" Tom asked.

"I said you're probably right. Bet her car is a mess."

As James' cruiser snaked around the hairpin curves of Cline Road, they looked for Abby's car or any sign of the wreck. Overgrown weeds were so tall they reached over and brushed the sides of the car with each slight breeze. It was as though someone had planted the head-high grass so it would grow, precisely, to meet the ruts in the two-lane dirt road. Tom commented about how different the road looks in June compared to when he was last here in November.

James agreed. "And I don't think I've ever driven it when I wasn't in a hurry to reach the house. It's like a maze and I'm always concerned about meeting another car and having to pull off the ruts and go through sand and weeds." That must happed a lot, James thought.

"You think that's what happened to Abby?" Tom was glancing back and forth, searching for her car when the narrow path opened to the entrance to the big old house on the hill.

"I guess we can ask the Lord of the Manor, himself." James pointed to Theo, who was standing on the front porch.

Theo met them half way down the steps.

"Evening, James – Preacher. How's Ms. Rials doing?"

"She's resting, Theo." James kept his composure in check as he spoke. "I decided to stop by and see, for myself, exactly what happened. By the way, where is Abby's car? We looked for it coming in."

"Oh, you wouldn't be able to see it from the road." Theo motioned for them to follow him to the back of the house. "I been tellin' the boys to get the bush hog out there and cut down those weeds aside the road so folks can see where they're goin'. But they don't listen to me since they got grown. Actually, they ain't never listened to me." He chuckled and kept walking.

"Where are we going, Mr. Cline?" James asked.

"I though you wanted to see the car." Theo turned and pointed to the barn, the largest of several old outbuildings behind the main house.

James was surprised to see Abby's car inside the barn, still jacked up and suspended from the wench of a tractor. "Why did you move it?"

"Well, I couldn't let it sit there with the top down; what with all the rain showers we've had lately. Least I could do was take care of the little lady's car after she ran off the road and hit that tree like she did, even if she won't hurt bad."

Up to this point, Tom had stayed quiet but he jumped suddenly at Theo and shouted. "Why in the world didn't you call 911? Are you crazy?"

James put his hand on Tom's shoulder and pulled him back. "What Tom means, Theo, is that it is always safer to call for help when something like this happens. And, you're never supposed to move an injured person." He pushed Tom behind him and safely away from Theo.

"I'd like to take a look at her car now."

"Sure. Come on in boys." Theo slid the barn doors open and turned on the lights. "Hang on while I set her on the ground." He jumped inside the cab of the tractor then lowered the car and unhooked the chain.

They circled the car, looking for damage. Other than sand and weeds imbedded in the wheels and undercarriage, the only visible body damage was a broken right headlight and a dented bumper. It was getting late, near sundown, which made it difficult to see the car where it sat. James decided they should return the next morning for a better look.

James took notes, saying it was necessary since Theo did not call 911. That was a lie, of course and he hoped Theo did not notice.

"We will be back around seven tomorrow morning." James told Theo as they walked away. "We need to finish getting your statement and make sure your boys are here. I need their statement, too. And, I'd better find Abby's car just where it is now."

James stopped by the cruiser and turned back to Theo.

"I'd sure hate to think you or your boys had planned to hide that car – make like someone stole it. Then sell it, maybe? Or strip it and sell it for parts?"

"Good Lord, James." Theo feigned innocence. "You know me, James."

"Yes, Theo. I do know you." James replied as they drove away.

James and Tom arrived back at the hospital in time to sit down with Rachel and the doctor who explained Abby's injuries.

"I'll make sure she stays comfortable through the night. Tomorrow," he said, "we will start making plans for surgical repairs."

When James questioned the wait, Dr. Hall said he wanted-ed to make sure there was no further internal bleeding or swelling of her brain. He slapped James on the shoulder and said, "Don't worry. She will be fine – eventually. However, she has suffered some tough injuries that will take time to heal.

The process can't be rushed."

James spent the night outside the Critical Care Unit, watching television while stretched out on the couch. He got no sleep. Instead, he watched the clock, wishing away each incredibly slow four-hours between bedside visits. The Critical Care Unit was where hospital visiting hours became visiting minutes, fifteen to be exact. James used those precious minutes to watch her sleep. He kissed her cheek and told her that from this point on he would be her protector and always keep her safe.

It was a long night but by daybreak, he had developed a plan, one that started with a trip to the cabin.

"Sorry you have to come in on your day off." James gave Rachel a hug.

"I wouldn't be anywhere else this morning. Remember, before you met her, Abby was my best friend. She's like a sister to me." Rachel would stay by Abby's side but gave James a suggestion before he left. "When you get to the cabin, please take a shower."

It was ten minutes to seven when he and Tom made it to Cline Road. James hoped his clean uniform and no-nonsense professional attitude would strike a bit of intimidation among the Clines. He did not want to scare them off but this morning he wanted everyone to see him as the Sheriff's Deputy, not Abby's fiancé. James stressed to Tom the importance of his role of silent assistant in this investigation. He was not to interject thoughts or emotions into this visit.

"Tom, please, I need you to just be a witness, okay?"

Tom nodded in agreement but truth was James wished

he had come alone. His training and experience gave him the confidence to, safely, do his job alone. However, having a layperson riding with him was a distraction he did not need, especially one like Tom. Lately, Tom's actions were becoming unpredictable. That was something James had noticed in the war room. There he could be quiet, seemingly uninterested for hours then change in a flash into an unrecognizable bully. It was as though Tom had developed a Dr. Jekyll and Mr. Hyde personality. Although Tom had been quiet on the ride this morning, James feared the possibility the Mr. Hyde could show his face if things did not go well this morning.

All three men were waiting outside the barn when the cruiser pulled up. James opened the glove box and handed Tom a camera.

"I forgot to tell you. I need you to take pictures of the car while I'm asking questions – you don't mind, do you?"

"Consider it done." Tom seemed pleased to have an official job.

"Morning Boys – Theo." James barely gave them time to respond. "Now, which one of you wants to go first?" James motioned towards the cruiser with the motor running. The air conditioner kept the makeshift interrogation room cool, for James benefit more than the Clines' comfort.

"Come on guys. Now don't be shy. Nolan, why don't you go first? It won't take but a minute." James walked back to the cruiser hoping Nolan interpreted his question as a statement, even a demand. It must have worked. Nolan followed like the proverbial lamb.

"Hey, James?" Theo called from the barn. "What's all this picture takin' about?"

"Crime scene photos, Theo." James quipped, and then added, "Haven't you ever heard of taking pictures for insurance purposes?" He turned back to Nolan and added, "That reminds me, you don't object to being recorded, do you?" James did not wait for a response but continued to the car. Again, Nolan followed like a shadow.

Taking statements from all three Cline men took less than an hour and the trip to the scene of Abby's fender-bender took about the same. The information told James nothing. It seemed the accident itself was, indeed minor. If not for the act of the Clines moving her, she would only have suffered a bump on her head. James would have to concede that, while he wished he could arrest the Clines for assault, it was not going to happen. Last time he checked, stupidity was not a crime.

As they prepared to leave, James got a call from dispatch. Rachel called to say Abby was about to go into surgery. She was awake and asking for him so he should get back to Rose County Medical as soon as possible if he wanted to see her first.

On the drive back, Tom was talkative. He was so excited it was hard to believe he was the same man who remained calm and quiet throughout the entire visit. It was a though he had held it in as long as he could.

"So, what did you think? What did they say happened? I think I got some good pictures of the car." He asked questions in rapid succession.

"I can't wait to get these developed so we can analyze them in the war room. " He added. "I hope they give us some answers."

"I don't think we're going to get any answers – none we can use anyway." James knew there may be more to how Abby received her injuries but he could not think about that now and he would not question her about it until she was better.

"Seems pretty straightforward to me." Tom sounded confident. "Abby was just careless. She should never have been there. Little Miss Know-it-all got in way over her head this time." Tom was still talking.

James was on the verge of yelling at Tom. *Isn't blaming Abby for this like blaming Jessica Cline for her own murder?* James kept his cool, though, for Abby's sake. They had just pulled into the hospital parking lot.

Before getting out of the cruiser, Tom put his hand on James' shoulder, instantly transforming from a manic-depressive amateur photographer back into a beloved Baptist preacher. He closed his eyes ad bowed his head.

"Let's take a minute to pray."

James brushed Tom's hand from his shoulder. "No." He was halfway to the hospital door when he came back to add, "I don't want to pray with you, Tom. I want you to shut the hell up. I just want to see Abby."

What happened next was a blur.

It would be nearly five hours before James was once again in his car, alone with his thoughts, his happiness that Abby's surgery went well and his disappointment at his actions towards Tom. It was hard to make sense of what had happened. Perhaps two stressful days without sleep had caught up with him, clouding his judgment. Getting angry was one thing, but losing it to the point of assaulting a preacher was something he never thought himself capable of doing, However, that was exactly what had happened right there, in the parking lot of Rose County Medical Center.

⁂

Rachel wiped dried blood from around the cut above Tom's eye. It had run down his cheek, making the injury look worse than it was. Still, he winced when Rachel applied pressure.

"Damn it! Hold still. You're acting like a child." She scolded him then stood back to examine the cleaned wound. "It's not too bad but you're going to need stitches – maybe two or three."

She gathered suture supplies, anticipating what the emergency room doctor would need to sew up the cut. She worked in silence, making it hard for Tom to tell whether she was worried about him or angry that he was an extra patient in her emergency room.

"Now, tell me again just how you fell to get this kind of cut on your head?"

"I told you. I tripped over the curb in the parking lot." Tom was trying to keep his story consistent with the last lie he told. "I must have blacked out when I fell. Next thing I remember was George calling my name." He pointed to the security guard still standing at the door.

"That doesn't sound right to me." Rachel leaned over and kissed his uninjured cheek. "Something caused this. I have never seen you just fall for no reason. Did you have a dizzy spell? Maybe your blood sugar dropped. What have you eaten today?"

Tom could tell she would not stop until she found a

reason for his injury.

"That's probably it," he said. "I haven't eaten much today."

He could not bring himself to tell her what really happened in the parking lot. Heck, he was not sure if he even knew.

A young intern came in, examined his wound, and shook his head. "Wow, you're going to have a headache, for sure." After closing the cut with three tiny stitches, he instructed Rachel to watch Tom for a couple of hours before taking him home.

"I don't think this is bad enough to suspect complications, so no x-rays today." He handed Rachel a prescription. "That is, unless he exhibits strange behavior in the next two hours."

Tom wanted to laugh at that, but it hurt to laugh. *Strange behavior? Good Lord! If that barely-wet-behind-the-ears doctor only knew!*

Even though Tom's memory was still a little fuzzy about the incident, he was clear about who hit him. James hit him. Tom was certain about who caused it, too. Jessica Cline caused it.

She had been a voice in his head almost a year now. She moved in the day Tom wrote her eulogy, in hopes it would help her rest in peace. That did not happen. Instead, from the day Jessica Cline locked herself in his psyche, she joined the other poor lost souls who had no one else to talk to but Tom. They were stuck, awaiting validation for their lives and vindication for their deaths. Most of the voices, such as Tom's mother, father, and little sister were content to be present but dormant, only reaching out for attention now and then. He had controlled them for years. However, when she joined the others, Jessica became the leader. Stronger and louder, she could force her way into Tom's thoughts anywhere, anytime. Perhaps, her manner of death empowered her and now, she was becoming difficult for Tom to control, especially at her home and around her family.

For the first time in nearly three days, James watched Abby's eyes scan the room as though she was searching for something familiar. She followed James' voice as he talked to her in soothing tones until she saw him ease himself beside her on the hospital bed.

"I'm here, Babe." James moved closer so she could see him better. He brushed her cheek with the back of his fingers for added reassurance. He shushed her when she tried to talk, reminding her, she was going to be fine but she had to rest. She tried to smile and almost made it before drifting off to sleep again.

He did not leave until she was sleeping soundly. He knew Rachel would be there soon but he did not want to see her until after he had spoken to Tom. James felt guilty and knew he must apologize, although Tom had it coming.

A loose-lipped nursing assistant told James about Tom's admission to the emergency room the day before. He got stitches before his discharge. He should be fine, she said. James decided to stop by the parsonage on his way to the lake.

"So, what brings you here, Deputy?" Tom was waiting by

the door by the time James knocked. His right eye was swollen shut with a thick white bandage plastered over his brow. Shades of black and blue filled the bridge of his nose and was starting to pepper down his cheeks.

"Geez, Tom. I didn't realize I clocked you that hard." James stopped short of an apology, not yet certain the preacher deserved one. "Can I come in? I think we need to talk."

Tom did not answer but walked into the kitchen. James followed. He was surprised to see Tom pull two beers from the fridge, open both then place one in front of James before turning the other up to his own lips.

"What?" Tom responded to James' unasked question. "It's time folks realized preachers and their families are human. We are not perfect. Some of us have wives who curse like sailors." He turned the bottle to his lips and sat the empty bottle back down on the table. "Beer is my vice. Hell, it beats those damned pain pills they gave me."

"So, James, why did you do this to me?"

"I came here to ask you the same thing, Tom." James realized this visit was not going to end well.

He took a chance on calling Abby's hospital room, hoping a nurse would pick up. Instead, Rachel answered after just one ring.

"Just checking in." He tried to sound nonchalant. "How's she doing?"

"Really good. A little clear liquid dinner – we might try some solids tomorrow."

James interrupted. "Has she said anything about the wreck?"

"No, she can't remember a thing but it's still early – oh,

just noticed the time. I have to go. I will tell her you will be here in the morning. Okay?"

James stopped her. "Wait. I stopped by to check on Tom today."

"Thanks, James," Rachel said. "I'm sure he appreciates that."

"Rachel, can we get together and talk sometime tomorrow? Just to catch up."

"Sure. How about lunch at this delicious place I know – the hospital cafeteria? Say 11:30?"

"Sounds good." When James hung up the phone, he poured himself a drink and settled into the recliner. The fitting words of "My Girl" came from the radio, reminding him that Abby was the most important thing in his life. Tomorrow he would remind Rachel of that and let her know that from this point on Abby's recovery, not some cold case murder, would be his only mission.

"I had lunch with James today." Rachel made small talk while removing Tom's bandage then stepped back to view his wound. "I think you can leave this off now – let it get a little air. You can cover it Sunday if you feel self-conscious in front of the congregation."

"I don't know if I should try to preach this week. What if they think there is something wrong with me. I'm sure, by now, everyone has heard how clumsy I am." Tom shrugged.

"That's ridiculous. You have had so many calls from concerned members this week. They will just be happy to see you're okay." She said.

"Like I said, James and I had lunch today. Just to catch up. He seems to think that we should take a little break from the murder case." Rachel saw Tom's shoulders stiffen. She could tell he was not happy.

She repeated their lunchtime conversation, explaining that for now, Abby's recovery and rehabilitation was James' main concern. He knows it will be lengthy but wants to spend every minute helping her heal as quickly and thoroughly as possible. Until then, Abby's care and James' job will leave no time for the war room. Finally, she said James thinks Tom needed a hiatus from the investigation, as well. Rachel could tell that Tom was not pleased.

"I guess you feel the same way?" Tom asked.

"I guess I do." She answered.

Her words seemed to trigger anger in Tom's voice. He slammed his fist onto the table and glared at his wife.

"Did he tell you that was his only reason for wanting to back off the investigation? I bet he did – I knew it. I was right about James all along. He can't be trusted, Rach." Tom paced around the kitchen, his anger turning to rage.

"What makes you think that?" She asked.

"Did your young, handsome lunch date tell you he was the one who did this to me?" Tom pointed to the stitches over his eye.

Rachel was speechless.

"That's right." Tom shook his head and yelled. "He didn't like me suggesting that Abby shouldn't have gone to the Clines alone. She should have waited for you or called me before going to that place. That made James mad. So mad he hauled off and punched me in the eye." Tom could see

203

Rachel was tearing up.

"And then, he just left me lying there and drove off."

It was early morning when Rachel banged on the cabin door. She hardly slept anticipating her visit to Clark Lake and the dialogue she and James would have. She banged again, louder this time. James was surprised to see her.

"Rachel, what's wrong? Why are you here? Is Abby okay?"

"Damn you, why didn't you tell me?" She pushed past him and plopped onto the couch. "Why did you hit my husband? What's wrong with you — and why did you leave him like that?"

James let Rachel rant while he poured them each a cup of coffee.

She took a sip then repeated Tom's explanation of James' assault.

"Hitting him was a shitty thing to do. You could have killed him – I'm ashamed of you!" Rachel shook her head. "And all because Tom was concerned for Abby's safety."

"I know." James admitted. "I never should have done it – and I am ashamed and I will tell him so. But... did he tell you the rest?"

He could tell by Rachel's expression, he had not.

"I started getting angry when Tom said she was trying to solve the murder by herself. But when he told me, she had it coming and he would not be surprised if she had offered them sex for information and wound up getting beat up when she tried to get away, that's when I clocked him." Rachel wanted to call James a liar but she knew he was telling the truth.

15.

April 6, 2000
James Wilcox

It had been a long eight months. Even so, thinking back, James had to wonder how so much could happen in such a short time. Abby's accident and recovery, the loss of her career and the discovery of a new one were too many events to go through in less than a year. Most had started as tragedies but ended in blessings. He hoped that the happiness gained this year would pale in comparison to the special event about to happen. Today, Abby would become his bride.

Looking out the window towards the lake, the vine-covered trellis caught his eye. Yesterday, he had moved that trellis six times before Abby was happy with its placement. It had to be in the perfect spot for every guest to see the beauty of Clark Lake from every angle. Next, she gave every chair the "seat test", positioning each one so every attendee would have the perfect view of the ceremony and its trellis-framed lake view. It had taken nearly two hours but now, as he prepared to make his way to the altar, walking by all those perfectly seated friends and family, James realized Abby was right. The setting was beautiful. He was glad he went along with everything she asked. His bride-to-be deserved to have exactly the kind of wedding she always imagined.

Before walking out the door to be married, James took a moment to reflect on his love for Abby and the struggles to make today happen.

Seeing Abby make such progress in a little more than six months was a miracle James would not have believed had he not been there to experience it with her. Somehow, she had healed from a ruptured spleen, shattered kneecap, broken arm, fractured ribs, and a concussion. He knew that had not come from a minor fender-bender and knew there was more to the story. However, Abby remembered nothing and the Clines were saying nothing.

Once home from the hospital, she made wonderful progress with care from the team of home health workers, supervised by Rachel and James. When she was stable, James proposed and Abby accepted, with one stipulation. "No more investigations." After losing her job with the FBI, thoughts of solving anything seemed bittersweet.

"I've lost enough. I don't want to lose my best friend, too." She said.

For James, that was it. Abby's wish was his command and, from this day forward, James vowed to leave the past in the past. Jessica Cline's murder would remain a cold case for someone else to solve. While the bond between Abby and Rachel could never be broken, the friendship between James and Tom remained guarded.

When he reached the altar, James shook hands with Omar, who served as Best Man. Tom would perform the ceremony and stood, facing the guests and clutching his Bible. James gave him a cordial nod as he took his place and turned to face the aisle. As the string quartet began to play Vivaldi's Four Seasons, everyone turned their attention to the cabin porch and to Abby who stood at the top of the steps. She was beautiful and her radiant smile brought a slight, but noticeable gasp from James.

Matron of Honor, Rachel was first down the aisle. She smiled and winked at James before focusing on Tom. She held a pageant-like smile but kept her eyes locked on her husband. James wondered if she might be concerned about what Tom might say or do during the day's festivities.

Tom motioned for everyone to stand when Abby descended the steps. She walked down those stairs as though she was never injured and when James stepped into the aisle halfway to take her hand, warm-hearted chuckles broke out among the crowd. Someone whispered, "How cute. He's so anxious, he's meeting her half way." Abby was surprised but took his hand and shook her head as if to remind him that was not in the script. James did not care. Reaching out to help her was, by now, instinctual.

For the next fifteen minutes, they exchanged vows, rings, and a kiss. All of it according to Abby's script.

The wedding party followed the recessional back into the house to complete the official documents while the guests followed a lighted footpath to the cocktail area where an open bar and hors d'oeurves awaited. Later, there would be dinner and dancing for the bride and groom and their three hundred-plus guests.

The locals were just getting to know Abby but James, having lived here all his life, knew just about everyone in town. That fact alone made limiting the guest list nearly impossible and that was fine with Abby. With Rachel and Tom being her only "family", Abby thought it fitting to invite nearly the entire population of Eden Falls. It appeared they all showed up, too.

After a few more wedding pictures, the couple joined their guests under the tent on the side lawn. After the traditional introductions, Tom stood to give a speech. James held his breath but relaxed when the preacher delivered sincere and perfect words of happiness to the couple. All had gone well. The weather, the ceremony, and the reception, all were flawless. Even the band, James favorite, had been Abby's last minute surprise to James. They played a mix of oldies, beach and country music, something for everyone and the guests danced the night away.

The couple looked back and waved as they left for their honeymoon in a 1964 Mustang convertible. As they drove off, guests lined the drive, cheering and waving hand-held sparklers that reflected like diamonds across Clark Lake.

Mr. and Mrs. Wilcox were on their way.

Abby was happier than she had ever been. Five days with James on a Caribbean beach had been her request for their honeymoon. She picked the Caribbean because she had never been there and just five days because her job with *The News Tribune* would start the Monday after their return home.

Lord knows, they both deserve a vacation. The entire past year had been a roller coaster ride, chaotic and, at times disorienting. There were still blocks of time Abby could not clearly remember. Doctors had said that may be due to her concussion and may return with time. However, with each month post-rehab she marked off the calendar, Abby worried about it less and less. Suspending the murder investigation had helped, as well.

Even, with all the problems of the past year, Abby knew this had been the luckiest year of her life. She had a happy future to embrace along with James, her very own "twofer", who came to her rescue in more than one way.

Not only had James cared for her physical needs until she healed, he kept her from wallowing in self-pity when she lost her FBI job before it even began. He encouraged her to apply for the position of newspaper reporter even when she did not feel qualified and was waiting at the door with champagne and roses when she rushed in to tell him the *Tribune* had hired her.

He was her protector, mostly keeping her safe from herself and her new surroundings. During walks around the lake to strengthen her legs, he taught her how to identify poison ivy and, until she became proficient at spotting it, he pointed out what plant to rub on her skin to take away the itch. He taught her the areas of Clark Lake to best avoid stumbling on a cottonmouth, much like pointing out which parts of Rose County were too dangerous to travel through alone. James was a good teacher, never condescending. He did not hover. Abby had been a good student, too, always listened and, usually, took his suggestions.

Only once had Abby seriously doubted the validity of James' request. When she asked that she distance herself from Tom and Rachel he sounded more like a jealous teenager than an adult with legitimate concerns for her safety.

That had been the only time they ever fought to the point of nearly calling off their engagement. Rachel was like her sister and Tom, her big brother. They were not just her surrogate family, they were her only family and she was not ready to jeopardize that relationship. Even after James pointed out Tom's growing erratic behavior, much of which she missed during recovery, Abby doubted him.

Of course, Abby remembered Tom's dramatic mood swings and his growing obsession with finding Jessica Cline's killer. He was just a passionate right-fighter, she thought. It was not until Rachel confided in Abby about her own fears that Tom was headed for a nervous breakdown did she re-think her opinion.

"Abby, Tom knows he's sick but he can't help it. He tries to hide and control it but, he knows." Rachel pulled a tissue from her purse as she talked, "Abby, I have to tell you something but please don't tell anyone, not even James." She was starting to scare Abby.

"For weeks now, I've been helping Tom write his sermons. So far, I don't think anyone has noticed; at least no one has said anything — but this can't go on. Tom needs help – professional help but he knows the Deacon Board will fire him if they even suspect he has mental problems. Tom loves this job. Losing it would kill him!"

"Abby, he has asked me to help him draft a letter to the Board requesting time off for a sabbatical, a mission trip of sorts." Rachel stopped and took a deep breath.

"It's a lie, I know but he will not get help any other way. I have rationalized things by telling myself that this really is, in a way, a sabbatical. It's a mission trip to get my husband well again." Rachel squeezed Abby's hand as she spoke.

"You know Tom's a good man and an amazing minister. We just want a chance for him to heal and come back to his job, his calling. I have contacted his old doctor at Sheppard-Pratt Psychiatric Hospital in Maryland in hopes they will admit him again. He agrees with me, he thinks we've caught it in time – like before."

Rachel's words still rang in her ears...*admit him again?.. his old doctor?...caught in time?* Abby knew her memory was not that bad. When had all that happened and why had Rachel kept it from her?

Abby remembered that conversation as the turning point that made her realize she should always trust James. Yet, she did not question Rachel. Perhaps she was too shocked. She even went so far as to promise to keep Rachel's secret. She did, too, until today.

The newlyweds settled in for the three-hour flight to Raleigh. James noticed how quiet Abby had been all morning but he assumed it was just nerves about starting her new job in a few days.

"Okay, what's wrong?" He kissed the back of her hand. "I know it's a downer to leave five days in paradise to face the drudgery of married life in a cabin in the woods."

Abby stopped him. "Stop it. You know I love our beautiful cabin in the woods. It's not that. I have something to tell you – a secret I've been keeping."

"Oh, no." James slapped his forehead. "Don't tell me you're already pregnant." He was teasing her but when she looked at her watch and asked if it was too early to ask the flight attendant for a drink, James knew she was worried.

"My secret is not about us but it is serious. I almost told you before the wedding but I didn't want to stress you out even more than you were already. I would have told you this week but I didn't want to ruin our perfect honeymoon, so, it must be now. I do not want to start married life harboring secrets."

James listened as she shared her conversation with Rachel and their plan to deceive the Deacon Board. She shared how betrayed she felt by Rachel keeping this from her and how ashamed she felt for keeping the secret.

"I really thought I knew everything about Rachel and Tom. She never told me this happened before. I guess I was blind to the real Tom and I, sort of, feel sorry for Rachel. I knew she was worried about him. After all, that is why I came here. I knew he was eccentric but I did not know he was crazy."

James stopped the flight attendant and ordered them each a Bloody Mary. She gave a disapproving look and checked her watch. "I know it's nine in the morning. We haven't had breakfast."

He turned his attention back to Abby. "I get it. You're hurt. I understand why you kept her secret. Rachel is your best friend and she and Tom have treated you like family for years. Now you have me. I am your family." James hugged her and added, "We can't fix other people's problems, no matter how close we are to them. All we can do is support them from afar – whatever the outcome."

When James looked up the flight attendant had their

drinks on the cart. He handed Abby hers and said, "Here, drink your breakfast."

By the time they heard the landing gear drop, Abby's mood had improved and she knew it had little to do with the alcohol. There was a time when Abby envied Rachel for finding Tom, her perfect man, her "twofer". Now, she knew Tom was not perfect and Rachel was not the lucky one. James was the real "twofer".

The cabin was quiet with all signs of wedding festivities cleaned and cleared. The walls of each room had sticky notes attached explaining what was where in case something was out of place. This meticulous attention to detail was Rachel's work. Abby knew her friend was the only person whose organizational skills matched her own, another common personality trait that made them close. Both women were, without a doubt, neat freaks. Happier times, she thought.

Rachel had left one last note taped to the bathroom mirror, a throwback to their college days when class schedules sometimes caused the roommates to go days without seeing each other. If either of them found a note on the bathroom mirror, they knew it must be important. When Abby found the note, sealed in an envelope with her name written in Rachel's hand, she knew this note held the same level of importance.

When James brought their luggage into the bedroom, he found Abby, sprawled across the bed, reading the letter. She passed it to him. "Read it out loud."

A key fell out of the envelope as he unfolded the letter.

"Dear Abby," it began.

"By the time you read this, Tom and I will be in Maryland.

The morning of your wedding, the hospital called to say they would accept him. The Deacon Board approved his request for a sabbatical the previous Sunday, so the timing was perfect. Please forgive me for not telling you until now. I did not want to distract you from your big day.

"I will call you after I get Tom settled. I will be staying in a hotel near the hospital. The Board will use lay ministers until Tom returns, hopefully in September. I had everything from the war room boxed and moved to a storage unit. The key is enclosed. The storage room contents are yours to do with as you please.

"Love to you both,
Rachel"

16.

October 14, 2000
Abby Wilcox

James pulled back into the driveway. He put the car in park but left the engine running. He shouted out the window to Abby. "Do you remember where you put it?" He was talking about the key to the storage unit.

"Of course. Sit tight. I'll be right out." Abby answered.

They had been so busy since the wedding, making it easy to ignore the contents of the storage unit. Abby's new job made that easy, too. She loved working at *The News Tribune*. Her coworkers were great and many were becoming friends away from the desk. She had gained confidence in her reporting skills and decided journalism may just be her true calling even if it had come to her by default. James' work life had been hectic, too. A couple of months ago he received a well-deserved promotion to Lead Detective. He worked long, odd hours but loved it.

They both had been just too busy to think about that storage unit. Had it not been for Rachel's latest bi-weekly phone call, they probably would not be rushing to get there now.

"Guess what?" Rachel could not contain her excitement.

"Tom and I will be home in two weeks." She gushed on about how great he was doing and how she had been right. The doctors had caught his problems in time. Now, it was as though Tom's nervous breakdown never happened. She had the old Tom back.

Abby tried to act as excited as Rachel sounded. It would after all, be good to see her after six months yet it was hard to find the words. It did not matter. Rachel did not seem to notice.

"I'm sorry, Abby, but I need another favor. Can you stop by the parsonage just to check on things for me? The church has been sending the cleaning service once a month – and I really appreciate it, but you know how meticulous I am about my house. I know I can trust you to make sure it's perfect for me to bring Tom back home to. Oh, Hell listen to me! You're as big a neat freak as me." Rachel laughed and added. "You do still have your key don't you? Damn. I'm never going to be able to repay you for all this – uh oh, Tom's calling me. I've got to go."

"Wait!" Abby shouted into the phone. She wanted to tell Rachel how much things in Eden Falls had changed in six months. She wanted to remind her that she never asked how Abby was. She wanted to tell her she hoped their friendship could survive but she said none of that.

Instead, she said, I'm anxious to see you, too. I have something to tell you."

"So tell me now."

"No, not on the phone. It's a secret." Abby sent her love to Tom before saying goodbye.

She dreaded to tell James they had to make a trip to the

storage unit. However, she was, suddenly, clear about what to do with the contents. They would bring the boxes back to Clark Lake and make a huge bonfire. They would roast hot dogs and marshmallows and celebrate their giant purge. Ridding themselves of the sadness of the past, they would exorcise Jessica Cline from their lives and make way for a happy future.

When she told James of her plan, he thought it was a great idea. As he was leaving the room, Abby grabbed his hand and placed it on her stomach.

"Feel that?" She whispered. "He's kicking."

17.

May 8, 2001
Wesley Cline

The day began in turmoil when Theo refused to drive Wes and Nolan to Pop's store, claiming he was not wasting the gasoline in his truck just so their sorry asses could stay drunk. If Theo's hands were not shaking and he was refusing to drive them to Pop's, Wesley knew what that meant. Theo had a bottle hidden somewhere nearby and he would not be sharing it.

Nolan had stomped out of the house earlier, grumbling profanities at no one in particular. He was, most likely, in search of a drink to cure his own ills. His juvenile act of slamming the door had become his signature sound that amplified his lack of wellbeing. That's when everyone in the Cline house knew that Nolan would soon be in full-blown delirium tremens.

Thirst was Wesley's first sign of withdrawal and he knew from experience that water would help postpone the inevitable. This morning he downed a full glass then held it under the kitchen faucet for a refill. As the cool liquid trickled down his throat, it created a wonderful feeling to sooth his scorched esophagus. He savored the taste. One of the few things the Cline farm had going for it was great tasting well water. They were lucky that this well, dug nearly two hundred years ago, still produced such pristine and plentiful water.

With his back against the kitchen counter, he downed the second glass of water and reached over to set the glass in the sink. Betrayed by his own shaking hands, Wesley upset the stack of dishes on the counter. He knew the sound of crashing plates and silverware would rile his sleeping father so he braced himself for Theo's profanity-laced explosion. Nothing happened. He tiptoed across the kitchen floor towards the den and peeked around the door, curious as to why Theo had not been jarred awake from his early morning nap. Maybe the noise had scared the old man into a massive coronary and he was dead from the shock. As he peeped into the den, Wesley hoped to see his dad's lifeless body. Instead, Theo was sprawled on the sofa, not only still breathing, but snoring loudly. He smelled like whiskey, an odor that permeated the couch he occupied as well as the air around him.

"You shit-faced ole fart." Wesley wanted to kill Theo where he lay. It would be easy to smother him with a sofa cushion. No one would be the wiser. What Wesley wanted do was bash the asshole's head in with a hammer. That is what he deserved.

"And no one would blame me." Wesley stood over Theo and yelled to his face. Theo's only response was to smack his dry lips together and roll over. Now facing the back of the couch, his loud snoring returned.

"Good Lord, Wesley Cline! Don't scream at your Pa like that." His shouts had brought Myra to the den.

"Ma, you know, good as I do, this old fart never does

nothing around here 'cept get drunk. He won't even go to the store to help out his own sons. He never helps you out or fixes things when they break — hell, he sure won't work at a real job. He's just a worthless piece of shit!" Wesley returned to kitchen for more water.

"You need to watch your language in my house! And quit talking like that about your father. You know he always kept things nice around here until he got hurt." Myra continued her speech into the kitchen. "He always made sure his family was taken care of until the accident. Now he can't..."

Wesley interrupted. "Holy shit, Ma. Please. You remind me of that every day of my life. Okay, he was hurt! That was not my fault — yours neither. So, why does he take it out on us? You would have thought his legs got cut off instead of broke — and you know he was probably drunk when that tractor turned over on him. I would have guessed it ran over his head if I didn't know he was crazy as a loon before the accident ever happened."

When Wesley's voice became louder, Theo awoke, mumbling profanities and swinging his arms in a wild attempt to fight anything or anyone in his path. Disoriented, he stumbled and tripped over the only obstacles in his way, the coffee table and his own feet. Landing back onto the safety the couch, he passed out again. Wesley stormed out of the house, enraged and in search of Theo's source of inebriation. This time he was mad enough to tear into Theo's most prized possession, his old, always locked, truck.

It had been sitting at the edge of the hog pen for nearly five years. The tires had flattened long-ago and the rubber had rotted on one side. Weeds and briars had grown into the rusted fenders and a bush had conveniently sprouted under the front axle, growing just tall enough to hide Theo's narrow path to the driver's side door. Everyone knew Theo visited every few days, just to be alone with his coon dog, Buddy, and of course, a bottle. Select family members knew it had been his safe haven for years, others knew, but feigned ignorance. Sadly, close family members could have intervened, should have intervened. Myra certainly had the right to know what her husband was doing out there. Instead, she and the other passive-aggressive Clines chose to ignore the place Theo came to drink and escape his demons

A rusty metal pipe, picked up while walking down the path to the hog pen, was just the tool Wesley needed to unlock the old Ford. It proved effective with one swing to the passenger side window. He even smashed out the remaining headlight and side mirror, just because. Reaching through the broken window, Wesley opened the door and began to brush shards of glass from his seat. He had crawled over the piles of paper and trash on the center console before noticing the microscopic cuts on his hands. Tiny spots of blood bubbled up and grew fat as ticks before opening to trickle down his arms. As he wiped his bloody arm across his pants leg, he looked up and caught his reflection in the broken rear view mirror. A smug smile stared back.

The act of vandalism delighted Wesley. It was a thrill due, in part, to the promise of a much-needed drink. However, the added satisfaction of sticking it to Theo was nearly as intoxicating as a double shot of Everclear. He and Nolan had often dared each other to destroy the old truck, usually just after one of their squabbles with Theo, but it had always been an empty threat, one that neither brother thought was worth the consequences of such a dire act. Looking around at the results of today's activity, Wesley realized he could never un-ring that bell.

He looked around for booze but saw none. He sat on the torn leather seats and stared, in awe, at all the junk littered inside the cab. Before today, Wesley had never seen beyond the tinted windows. If he had, he probably would not have wasted the energy it took to break them.

"Nothing here but garbage and crap!" Wesley muttered to himself.

For years, Theo had his sons imagining there were stacks of money locked inside the old rust bucket. Wesley knew better than to believe that fantasy, but he figured there had to be something of value hidden inside. His first priority though, was to find a drink. Running his hands through the papers and trash on the floorboard, he felt a metal object beneath the passenger seat. It was wedged in so tight he could barely move it.

"Son of a bitch!" he shouted, repeatedly, while he pushed and pulled with all his might. When he heard the sound of glass bumping against metal and the heard liquid sloshing inside, he knew his imprecations had helped. Wesley worked at moving the metal wedge until he struck gold and uncovered a near-empty bottle of whiskey.

Fat drops of blood had started to trickle down his knuckles. It dripped onto old receipts, newspapers, and empty cigarette packs. His attention temporarily shifted to fashioning a makeshift bandage from a greasy pink cloth, probably used for long-ago oil changes. With the cloth wrapped tightly around his bleeding knuckles, Wesley returned to what was most important. He consumed the small amount of what must have been excessively aged liquid that remained in the Jim Beam bottle. Though barely enough to taste, it was enough to help calm his nerves.

It was getting late and Wesley knew he had better get out of Theo's, now-destroyed, truck. He would figure out how to stay away from him until he had made up a good lie about what happened. More importantly, he must find his next drink of liquor.

He remembered the metal wedge and reached back under the seat. No longer stuck against the liquor bottle, a little red box tumbled out with ease. It was only about four inches deep and nearly as rusted as the truck that was once its safe haven. A padlock, much too big for a box of that size was another, ridiculous looking level of security. Wesley wondered what kind of idiot would think to put such a contraption on a little old metal box. *One named Theo.* Wesley laughed aloud. *That big old silly-looking padlock is just the kind of thing Theo would do.*

Wesley had always tried to think like his father. It was a craft, honed in childhood, a method developed to outsmart Theo. He used it to protect his mother and to insure his own survival. If Theo had anything of value, Wesley knew he would hide it in just such a manner.

He wiped his bloody hands with another, easily found, dirty rag and tossed it aside. No longer worried about his wounds, Wesley's interest was now on his newfound treasure. He grabbed the box and slid back out the passenger side of the truck. He could just smell the cash inside. With the little metal box tucked safely under his arm, Wesley set out towards the shed to find a pair of bolt cutters.

With concerted effort and with blood still dripping from his hands, Wes managed to cut through the thick lock. When he realized the bolt cutter had done its job, he gave out a loud whoop, flung open the top, and dumped the contents onto the worktable. Old keys, two rusty bolts and an envelope was all the treasure he found. The name, "Jessie" was scribbled across the front of the envelope. Wesley recognized Theo's handwriting.

What the hell? Wesley held the envelope up to the light but could not see anything inside.

"Wesley...Wes!" Nolan was calling him. *Damit!*

He barely managed to stuff the envelope inside his shirt before Nolan came barreling into the shed, bottle in hand.

"Hey, Bro...Look what I found!" He handed a half-empty bottle to his brother, who took a long drink. Wesley never asked where the liquor came from — it was not important. They sank to the floor and passed the bottle back and forth until it was empty; brotherly love at its finest.

After a brief nap on the floor of the shed, Wesley woke to find his once-shaky hands calm. A mild headache and tenderness around the cuts on his hands were painful reminders of his attack on Theo's truck. Pulling himself off the floor, the rustling papers in his jacket brought another reminder. He stumbled over Nolan, who was propped against the wall, sleeping soundly. He never heard the shuffle of unfolding papers. Wesley leaned towards the doorway in search of better light but it was still too dark to read the fine print. He skimmed the documents but could only make out some of

224

the words clearly. ...*Adoption...Jessica Cline...authorization... DNA...paternity...*

Beads of perspiration began to form on Wesley's forehead and his shaking hands returned. This time, though, his symptoms had nothing to do with drinking. Wesley was now alert, stunned by a rush of dark memories that came pouring from the envelope along with its contents. *Why would Theo keep this? He promised to destroy it all. He promised!*

Stumbling over piles of trash and his still sleeping brother, Wesley ran out of the shed in search of better light to read the documents again. Perhaps the bright sun would change the words. *Is it possible to unsee something?* Maybe, if he found a safe place to look again, he would realize it had all been an illusion. *DT's does that kind of thing.* Clutching the papers tightly, he began to wander, unsure of his destination but certain he could not go home.

Hidden behind a tree, Wesley stopped long enough to catch his breath and unfolded the papers once again. Legalese — that was most of what he saw but did not understand; all the "parties of the first part", "whereas", and "hereafters" that filled the pages. Nevertheless, the words that made him sick to his stomach, the ones that referenced the paternity of his sister's baby, were still there for anyone to read and understand.

Caught in a trap of his own making, Wesley had no idea where to go or what to do. All he knew for sure was that he was a dead man. He was not even sure which sin Theo would try to kill him for committing: stealing the lock box or destroying his truck. Either one would be worthy of the death penalty in Theo's eyes but Wesley did not care anymore. Now, with his worst sins and deepest regrets exposed, he would go to jail, either for killing Theo or for incest.

For the first time ever, Wesley wished he had stayed in school. Then, maybe he could read and comprehend the legal documents in his possession. Nevertheless, he could not change that bit of history and, worse still, he didn't know anyone who could or would translate the documents. All he could think to do was to run, and when he reached the Cline farm property line, he ran into dense woods. Then, he ran some more.

It was getting late in the day and the sun began its drift towards dusk. When darts of sunlight shot through the branches of the trees on the horizon, Wesley followed them like the points of a compass. Flashes of super-bright lights caught his attention and he soon realized it was the sun glancing across the copper steeple of Bethel Baptist Church. The glistening spire was his answered prayer. He picked up his pace and sprinted across Highway 37, towards the church. Maybe this was divine intervention. If he were going to admit to something so heinous, he would rather confess to God than the authorities. Besides, he thought, maybe he could trust Preacher Tom.

The tap on the door had been so soft that Tom was not sure anyone was there. Perhaps the wind was rattling around the latch again, pulling the weathered screen door back and forth against the jam. He had grown accustomed to having to use the eyehook to keep the door from blowing open with every little gust of breeze that passed. He hit the mute button on the television remote and listened to hear another gentle rap. This time, he knew someone was knocking.

Tom was shocked to see Wesley Cline standing there, his back against the screen door, staring out into the night and looking around as though he expected someone to come sneaking up behind him. When he finally turned to face the preacher, the look on his face told Tom this was not a social call. He led the visitor into the kitchen.

"I need help, Preacher." Wesley pulled the now-crumpled papers from inside his shirt and held them out to Tom.

"What's this?" Tom's heart skipped a beat when he saw the envelope with "Jessie", handwritten across it. When he looked up, Wesley Cline stared at him, unblinking, giving Tom the time and the lighting to notice his sky-blue eyes encircled with yellow where the whites should be. They reminded Tom of his father. He had those same yellow eyes. Jaundice, Tom knew, meant cirrhosis, and death.

Wesley blinked, releasing a pool of tears that ran down his cheeks. He looked ready to collapse when Tom managed to ease his visitor into a chair. Wesley tried to speak through choked back muffled sobs, but his barely audible words made little sense.

"Just drink this and calm yourself down a bit." Tom handed him a large mug of hot coffee then poured one for himself.

As he sipped the coffee, trying to regain his composure, Wesley motioned for Tom to look at the papers. He watched Tom closely, as he opened the crumpled, dirty envelope to expose a familiar document, a copy of the same birth certificate Abby had discovered two years before. However, the adoption papers, held together with a rusty paper clip, were not copies but originals. Wrinkled and stained, the onion-skin papers were in sad condition as far as original legal documents were concerned but the signatures in blue ink proved them authentic.

"So, Wesley, what exactly is this you've brought me?" Tom hoped his demeanor did not give away his excitement.

It took two cups of coffee for him to gather the courage to verbalize why he was there but, at last, Wesley was finally able to speak.

"I found these papers in Pa's truck." He squirmed a little in his seat. "I figure, since I can't go back home no more, I might as well give this to you...and confess my sins about all this before I die." He hesitated, as if waiting for Tom's response.

It had been a long time since Tom had allowed himself to imagine this case solved, nearly three years. Everyone, even he, had given up on exposing the cover-up of Jessica Cline's murder. Once again, Tom felt those old stirrings, those feelings he used to get in the war room with each bit of evidence placed on a bulletin board. It was the same feeling one gets from finding an elusive piece to a giant jigsaw puzzle. But the piece that completed this puzzle, the one that provided a finished portrait of a murderer, remained missing. It was always the most important piece and, until today, remained the one never found.

"Preacher?" Wesley took on the appearance of a scared little boy, rather than the alcoholic brother of a murder vic-tim. He certainly did not resemble someone who was once the prime suspect.

"Wesley, we've all done things we're not proud of … you know, everybody's a sinner." Tom knew he had to choose his words carefully. "All we have to do is confess our sins to God. He forgives anything…but only if we acknowledge our wrongdoing." Tom paused then, in a soft voice, repeated, "Why can't you go back home, Wes? What did you do?"

"I can't go home 'cause I broke into Pa's truck and stole his stuff."

Wesley sounded like a worried teen. Still, he seemed to take note of Tom's skepticism and lack of understanding the seriousness of his transgression.

"No, you don't understand, Preacher. Pa has threatened us for years about messin' with his truck — not the one he drives, but the one he hides – the place he keeps his stash of booze and stuff. He has always said he would kill us for such — and he meant it. And, after finding this," he gestured to the papers, "I know he'd kill me, for sure."

Wesley stood and began to pace as he spoke.

"Oh, I busted up his truck all right. Glad I did it, too! That's why I have to leave — I'm going off somewhere — not sure where, but I wanted you to have these papers. I just want this off my mind. Somebody needs to know."

"Somebody needs to know what, Wesley?" Tom needed him to talk but not about leaving. "Tell me, what did you do that was so awful? You can trust me."

Wesley pointed to the papers. "Preacher, I've done some bad things in my life. I have drank more liquor than anyone can imagine, done drugs — every kind you can imagine. I have stole from just about everybody, including my own Ma. But the worst thing I ever did was hurt my little sister. I

229

know that now and I'm so, so sorry for it."

Tom could not tell whether Wesley's tears were falling due to remorse for his deeds or from the realization that he was caught.

"I didn't know it was a sin, I swear. When we started doin' it we were just fooling around, you know, playing doctor. We was just kids. I had seen Nolan do it to her, Pa, too. I hid outside the shed and watched 'em touch her. I wanted to see what it felt like and Jessie didn't seem to care. But then, I just couldn't help myself — I did more than touch, I held her down." His head and his voice lowered. "I went all the way."

With that, Wesley's confessions came pouring out and seemed unstoppable.

"Honest, I didn't know it was a sin but, I sure know now. It's all there — in that letter. Pa found out that we went all the way and, well then, she turned up pregnant. He told me he had taken care of it for me but I had to keep my mouth shut or he would turn me in. And he's always held that over my head in case I did something really stupid...like break into his truck." The slight tremble in Wesley's hands was starting to become more noticeable.

Tom motioned for him to sit back down, positioning himself between Wesley and the door. He did not intend to let him go until he got the most important confession, the one he had waited three years to hear.

Come on. You are almost there. Just say it. You killed her. I already know all about the incest in your crazy family. Just say it. Tell me you killed your sister, you sick bastard! The thoughts were his own but the voice Tom heard, guiding those thoughts, belonged to those from the past. They were the same voices that had been silent for more than a year. Now, after a three-month "sabbatical" at Sheppard-Pratt Hospital and the threat of losing his wife and his church, they were back. Tom had suspected they never really left. They were just hiding, waiting for a moment like this. He hoped he was strong enough to keep them under control.

Once again, Wesley stood to leave and Tom noticed the shaking hands of impending DT's. Tom pushed the voices away and led Wesley towards his study. Settling him on the sofa and covering him with a throw. Tom realized his own hands were trembling nearly as bad as his visitors were.

"I think I have just what you need." Tom pulled a bottle of Jim Beam from his desk drawer and held it up.

"What the ...?"

"I know what you're thinking." Tom confessed as he poured a shot and steadied Wesley's hand to grasp the cup. Tom poured another shot but set this one on the desk within his visitor's view.

"Preachers don't drink. Well, I'll keep your secret if you keep mine." Tom said as he placed a pillow behind Wesley's head and suggested he rest for a few minutes before leaving.

From behind the desk, he watched as Wesley relaxed and his tremors eased. Within minutes, Wesley had nodded off and Reverend Tom poured himself a drink – just to settle his own nerves. He then downed another and proceeded to read the documents.

If only Rachel were here! Tom looked at the clock. It was just after eight. She had gone to her monthly book club meeting and was not due home for at least two more hours. The more documents he read the more excited he became.

There was a time, Tom knew, Rachel would have been anxious to share this discovery, but that seemed a lifetime ago. This past year, neither of them had talked about Jessica Cline nor had they dared hint about trying to solve her murder. The couple's sole efforts had been towards improving their marriage and living a so-called, normal pastor and wife lifestyle. Rachel was there for Tom during some dark times and he did not want to scare his wife again. He dared not call and interrupt the meeting, especially since they were meeting at Abby's house.

Rachel stood by Tom when he was sick. She even hung in there when the cemetery voices got so loud he could no longer function as Bethel's pastor. She proved her love by watching over him during his insidious decline into that mental abyss. She managed to protect him for a while with clever cover-ups. Rewriting and recycling his old sermons when his "preacher's block" hit, and filling in at meetings when he was too busy conversing with the dead, were just two of Rachel's temporary fixes that worked for a while. However, when Tom began to converse, openly, with the dead, not only Jessica Cline but Tom's own long-dead father, Rachel knew the outpatient psychiatric care was no longer appropriate. During one of Tom's infrequent periods of lucidity, she helped him draft a request to the Deacon Board for a sabbatical. Thankfully, the congregation gave their blessing for the requested "mission work".

Yes, it had been a lie but one they both felt justified in telling. Rachel convinced Abby and James of her belief in Tom. She knew her husband was a good preacher and it would be a shame she said for him to never grace the pulpit again.

That would surely happen if his mental health were in question. Abby and James supported her decision. Tom's time at Sheppard-Pratt Hospital in Baltimore was, in its own way, a true sabbatical; one that pulled the young minister from the brink of collapse and brought him back to mental clarity.

That all took place over a year ago and, while Tom thought about Jessica Cline now and then, he was no longer obsessed with finding her killer. He had not heard her voice, not even once, since he returned. Not until tonight when Wesley Cline knocked on the back door.

Again, he looked at the clock, wishing it were time for his wife to get home. He wanted Rachel with him to witness whatever Wesley had to say. Maybe she could help him figure out what he should do when Wesley confessed to Jessica's murder.

Tom was rereading the documents when Wesley awoke with a start.

"Preacher, I had a bad dream. Do you think I will go to hell for getting my sister pregnant?""

Tom was absorbed in the paperwork and did not look up.

"What?" Tom glanced back and forth, trying to reconcile Wesley's words with the papers he was reading. When Wes began to repeat himself, Tom stopped him, mid-sentence.

"Wesley, your name's not on any of this paperwork." Tom held up one of the documents for Wes to see. "Look! This is the birth certificate. Your name is not on it. It's blank."

Tom wondered why Wesley thought his name was on the birth certificate. Had he not even bothered to read it?

"Who told you that you fathered Jessie's baby?"

Wesley stared at the ceiling for a few seconds, as though

he did not know how to talk about it.

"Pa...Pa told me. He said I would go to jail if anybody found out. I know he would throw me out of the house if Ma ever found out and, he claimed she would be so ashamed of me that she would never speak to me again. And I knew he was right."

Tom interrupted. "You mean you never talked to anyone about this? Not even Jessie?"

"No. By the time Jessie got back home after having the baby, she was different. She was drinkin' bad and on drugs. I don't think she even remembered it. None of us talked about it — and that made it easy to, almost, forget it ever happened.

"Pa was the only one, aside from Senator Connors, who knew and they promised not to tell. They said, as long as I stayed quiet, they would protect me from the law. That's why I signed that paper."

"What?" Tom was even more confused. "You signed what paper, Wesley?"

"The land paper. They said if I signed over my farm acreage to Senator Connors, he and Pa would take care of me and make sure no one found out. But why would they do that if I'm not the daddy?" Wesley reached over for the glass of whiskey still sitting on the desk. He swallowed it in one gulp. Tom did not try to stop him.

A look of realization slowly settled across Wesley's face.

"Preacher, now I wonder if Pa was trying to protect me – or trick me. I bet Nolan's the one who got her knocked up." He slammed his fist into his palm and added, "That sorry bastard — bet that's why he up and joined the Army so quick."

"No. Noland did not father Jessie's baby." Tom was reading from a page labeled DNA Paternity Results. "Just sit down, Wesley. I think I know what happened."

Tom's thoughts were starting to become muddled. When that happened, it was hard to keep the voices from slipping back out. *Rachel, please come home. This is big news. I want to share it with you. I need your help.* With or without Rachel, Tom knew he needed to keep Wesley talking.

"Please sit back down. I'll try to explain what I've read."

Wesley complied and gave his full attention to Tom as he read from the document.

"It seems Theo paid Connors a visit after learning of Jessica's pregnancy, claiming Ashton had fathered the child. Theo was looking to blackmail the Senator, seeking either money or a shotgun wedding, and he was betting Connors would take the bribe. Turns out, he was right. Connors did not want that kind of publicity just before an election, so the good Senator apparently struck a deal with your Pa. He paid him off to keep quiet about the baby. Connors even paid for an out-of-state, non-traceable adoption."

Tom could tell Wesley was listening and, whether or not he fully understood any of it, he believed every word the preacher said. At some point, the voices infiltrating Tom's mind began to embellish the printed words. With a quick wave of the next document in front of Wesley, Tom claimed it was the agreement the two men had signed. That was a lie, but one that simply slid from the preacher's tongue like melted butter.

Continuing to pretend to read from the document, Tom made up facts as he went along. Somehow, even with no proof to back it up, Tom knew the words were true. *She* had told him. Jessica. She was here and Rachel was not. It was as if she had sneaked in the back door with Wesley. Now, she was back for good. At last, she would lead them to the truth, whispering thoughts in Tom's ear with every page her brother had brought him.

Tom reached over and poured another shot of whiskey and, irreverently, swallowed it in one gulp. He poured another and passed it to Wesley before continuing to speak.

"But then, Theo got greedy and, before long, the Senator grew tired of always having Theo's hand in his pockets, demanding more money at every turn. Connors needed more incentive, a better reason, to keep paying Theo so..."

Wesley interrupted Tom. "Now, I think I get it. That sorry bastard! Pa told me I was the daddy just so I'd give up my twenty acres of land." Wesley shook his head in disgust. "Now, ain't that a hoot? Pa was blackmailing Connors then Connors turned the tables. So, Pa blackmailed me. Damned if you can't get any sorrier than that."

"I'm afraid it gets worse." Tom turned the page of made-up information. It was like telling a bedtime story to a child. Except, Tom hoped this story would end in a murder confession.

"Theo's greed must have gotten out of hand or Connors just got tired of him because, according to this, Connors must have forced Ashton and Theo to take paternity tests. Looks like all payments stopped when DNA results showed Ashton was not the father."

Tom looked into Wesley's yellow eyes "You know what that means don't you?"

The color drained from Wesley's face. He jumped up and bolted to the door.

"Wesley! Where are you going?"

"Home." Wesley shouted back as he ran. "I'm gonna' kill that bastard!"

After finding his shoes and keys, Tom caught up with Wesley half way down Bethel Church Road and begged him to get into the car. It had been a challenge but he, finally, coaxed Wesley into accepting a ride home, encouraging him to talk and hoping he did not notice how slowly Tom was driving. His heart was racing and his head pounded with a kind of headache Tom had not felt in more than a year. He had not forgotten this kind of pain, though. The mental health professionals had called it an aura but Tom knew it as a familiar alarm, one that switched on that the voices in his head. With each new aura, the voices became stronger and harder to ignore. He struggled to will them away as he kept Wesley talking. Tom had no plan of action beyond this point but he knew it would not do to let the voices take over now. He must stay in control.

It was nearly nine o'clock when they began the winding drive up Cline Road. Tom's headache interfered with clear thinking. He had no idea about what would happen when they reached their destination. Wesley's non-stop curses about Theo became louder and more vitriolic. In a brief moment of clarity, Tom realized both he and Wesley were drunk, he from two shots, Wesley from the rest of the bottle. No good could come from that, Tom thought, although it had helped suppress the pain his head. He still wished Rachel were here to stop him from whatever was about to happen.

Wesley started jumping out of the car before it came to a complete stop, screaming Theo's name as he took the porch steps two at a time. Tom could barely keep up.

"Theo! Theo Cline! Get your sorry ass out here!"

Myra ran out of the house to meet Wesley on the front porch. "Your Pa's not here. He's doin' something at the shed, I think. What in the world is wrong, now?" She saw Tom standing by the car. "Preacher?"

Wesley sprinted down the steps and around the house running as fast as his wobbly legs could take him. Tom followed. He dared not lose sight of him since it was a dark, moonless, night and he had no idea where Wesley was leading him. He was thankful when they slowed down, which did not happen until they were well out of Myra's sight.

Both men were out of breath and neither spoke as they walked. Wesley led the way through the hog pen and past Theo's, now bashed up truck. Tom's heavy breathing could not drown out the swamp-like sounds of mud sloshing underfoot. Neither could it cover the sounds of men arguing, voices that seemed to emanate from the wooden structure about thirty feet away.

Wesley stopped and motioned for Tom to do the same. No problem, Tom thought as he bent over, hands on his knees, happy for the opportunity to catch his breath. He had not realized he was so out of shape. As his eyes adjusted to the darkness, Tom saw they had run a good distance. The lights from the Cline house were barely visible behind them, and his immediate surroundings were coming into focus. Old car parts and tires lay everywhere. An abandoned refrigerator was on its side, next to a rusty stove. The two appliances, it appeared, had landed a few feet short of the nearby woods where, as far as he could see, another dozen or so were scattered. The rest of the muddy landscape contained mostly garbage, identifiable solely by smell. Tom wondered how long it had taken to create this homemade landfill and tried to ignore thoughts of the kinds of small creatures that must be scurrying about.

Through a flickering light of the shed's half-open door, two figures came into focus. Tom recognized Theo and Nolan, two enraged drunks, squared off and ready to fight. Fists in the air, they lunged towards each other then, stumbled back, rocking and swaying around the perimeter of the shed like two confused prizefighters trying to land the perfect punch. As they moved each other around the eight by twelve foot wooden structure, they knocked against shovels and rakes leaning against the walls and kicked over buckets and boxes, anything in their path, all the while slurring profanities at each other.

Tom was about to ask what they should do, when Wesley charged towards the shed screaming, "I'm the one you want, you bastard! Nolan didn't bust up your truck, Ol' Man, I did!"

Before the shocked Theo could respond, Wesley dove onto the man, reaching for his throat with both hands. Nolan joined in the fight, as Tom stood, frozen outside the shed. What should he do? He could not bring himself to step inside, or intervene in any way.

Tom backed away, but only a few feet before stumbling over a tree root — or something that stopped him. He leaned against a tree, seemingly frozen in place, as the surreal, bloody scene unfold in front of him. All he could do was watch and listen as the action played out like a three-dimensional, pay per view event. As the Cline's fighting escalated, the voices in his head did, too. Jessica Cline's words won out.

Tom looked back towards the house. That was the place where Jessica Cline should have felt safe, the place where, even now, the only person who truly loved her sat, resting in her recliner, unaware, or unwilling, to stop the horror taking place so near. Completely out of sight, this shed was where Jessica's tormentors abused her for years. No one could see. No one could hear. Until this minute, no one cared enough to look.

The sound of breaking wood jolted Tom's attention back to the fight. It was Theo being body slammed against the workbench. He heard Wesley's voice, accusing Theo of incest and Nolan of the same. Theo was sprawled across the workbench, looking dazed and whipped. Clearly, his sons had gotten the best of him.

The voices coming from the shed and the voices speaking in Tom's head began their own war of words, spewing insults and accusations so quickly that Tom could not keep up. Soon, he could not tell who was real and who was dead. He stumbled back again, away from the shed door and started to run towards the lights of the distant Cline house to Myra, the only voice of reason he knew was close by.

When he turned to run, it happened. The confession he had waited years to hear. A voice had admitted to the heinous murder of Jessica Cline and the confession had been clear and concise. It sounded like Theo's voice. Tom turned again, lunging through the door of the shed.

"Get out, Preacher. You don't want to be here right now."

240

A near-breathless Theo held onto the doorframe to steady himself, trying to push Tom out the door.

"You're right, Theo. I don't want to be here." Tom had found his own voice and now felt he had an army behind him. The voices, silenced for a year, had resurrected to give him the strength to confront a killer.

With Jessica the loudest, the dead followed her lead, giving Tom powers he never before felt. The whisperers quoted subliminal scripture, giving Tom ability to do what he had always wished for, to speak in tongues. Louder and louder, the voices gave him the ability to spew foreign sounding imprecations towards Theo Cline.

Wesley, too, pushed Tom away, begging the preacher to hush. "He's mine!" Wesley kept saying. "Get out, Preacher. I'm already going' to hell — may as well take him with me!"

Wesley shoved Tom out of the way and lunged towards Theo but he was too late. With his back turned to his sons, Theo's outstretched arm had made contact with at long-handled axe that hung on the wall. Pulling it down and swinging wildly, he aimed for his sons.

"I should've killed you two sorry shits long ago." As he spat the words out, Theo's eyes grew wide making him look even more like the devil Tom knew he was. They were bloodshot-red and liver-diseased yellow, and they shot daggers of hate at his sons.

He threw the ax with all his strength but it missed his intended target. Instead, it struck the light bulb that hung from frayed wires in the rafters. When the bulb shattered, there was nothing but the pitch of darkness — but not for long. Naked electrical wires, swinging wildly overhead, tossed

241

sparks around the shed like an out of control firecracker on the Fourth of July. The final pyrotechnic display came from a nearby overturned gas can that ignited with a "swoosh". The escaped gas rolled across the old wood floor, sloshing gas into every crevice it found. It soaked into strewn trash, old newspapers, oil rags, and any up-till-now hidden legal documents and the sparks chased the trail of gasoline like a slithering snake that eventually struck with expected precision. Flames encircled the room, along with the fighting Clines and the preacher.

Leaping through a break in the flame, Tom ran towards the door but someone pulled him back inside. Theo tried to beat Tom to the only way out. Pushing and shoving, all four men tried to get through the small opening at once. Then, as if an unexplained hand reached into the shed and grabbed him, Tom found himself tossed to the ground, outside the wooden structure.

He managed to pull himself up to a standing position and could see through the growing flames that the Clines were still inside and still fighting. In a temporary return to clarity, Tom staggered towards the shed. *Someone should save them.*

The last voice Tom heard before his own collapse was that of Jessica Cline. "No!" she screamed.

Myra later reported that she had seen the flames from the kitchen window but by the time she managed to dial 911, the fire had sent black smoke billowing into a red-glowing sky. Ignoring her painful arthritis, she ran towards the cabin to save her boys. Once she got there, the fire had begun to die down but the heat stopped her from getting close. Myra squinted, but the smoke-filled air burned her eyes. All she could see was the silhouette of a man standing in front of the smoldering structure. Overjoyed that they may be okay, she called out.

"Wesley, is that you? — Nolan?"

Before she could call out again, the silhouette reached over and picked something up. She clearly saw a gas can. Through the wavy distortion of the fire, she watched him raise it high as though to toss it far away from the flames. Instead, Myra's heart nearly stopped when, she watched him turn and throw the gas can into the smoldering embers.

"This'll teach you, you bastard!" The man in silhouette screamed as the firebomb exploded, the ground shook, and Myra fell to the ground.

The man lay in a crumpled heap, conscious but moaning in pain when the fire trucks made their way up the narrow path followed by two patrol cars and an ambulance. Other than one man, there was nothing left to save. No big flames to fight either since the explosion had extinguished the fire.

The Sheriff stepped out of his car looking stunned. He learned that firefighters had pulled three bodies from the rubble. Omar was not surprised at the individuals involved in the tragedy but he was shocked at the person who started the fire. First responders said the man confessed at the scene. His injuries were minor.

"Damn!" was all the sheriff could say. Omar pulled Deputy Wilcox aside just as he had done three years before.

"Just when I thought nothing else bad could happen to

this family, I've been proven wrong."

They watched as the emergency vehicle transported Myra Cline to the emergency room. Understandably, she was in shock.

James Wilcox seemed to be in shock, as well. Omar knew that James would want to rush home to Abby. First, though, the Sheriff must ask James to accompany him to Bethel Church Road.

"Duty calls." James replied.

Omar hated it but, once again, they had bad news for a member of the Eden Falls community. This time, though, the bad news would include Rachel Kirby.

18.

October 23, 2005
North Carolina Central Prison
Abby Wilcox

S he shifted from side to side in the now-familiar but still-uncomfortable metal chair. Abby was just as anxious today, perhaps more so, than her first visit back in March. However, this time, it was not out of fear of the prisoner. She had learned to trust that the guard was, in fact, just outside the door for her protection and all she had to do was call out for his assistance. She had regained the confidence to contain or suppress her own insecurities at will. She had even learned to handle the prisoner's attempts to intimidate her at every turn. Yes, she had conquered many demons during the past seven months.

After regaining her proficiency to profile and her ability to revive her memory of instinctual training at Quantico, it had taken nearly a dozen visits to feel secure about interviewing this particular crazy prisoner. She had even been able to relax in this maze of rooms centered deep inside the inner sanctum of Death Row. It was work for Abby to overcome doubts about her ability to find the truth and it seemed like she was just beginning to make headway. She had thought – hoped — she would have more time to finish the project. However, this week's news had moved her self-imposed deadline up to today.

No longer could she afford to let the prisoner dole out information at a snail's pace as he had done every visit thus far. Abby was always aware that the prisoner was being manipulative, though she never let on. She usually managed to gain tidbits of information and side stories by allowing him to go on a tangent now and then, hoping to hear some accidental slips of detail that she could later explore. That would not work today. There would be no later. Time was up.

The heavy door swung open and the now-familiar sound of chains and locks striking concrete and metal played one last dirge as the prisoner was set for the interview. His raised eyebrows and the smirk on his lips told her this visit would begin just like all the others. He intended to be as difficult as always and it began with his usual diversionary tactic, a memory he suddenly recalled in a recent dream.

"She came to me, again, last night...and she stood in front of her brother's bedroom window...pointing..."

"Stop it!" Abby stood up and screamed at him, a move that must have taken the prisoner by surprise as he complied. He stopped talking and shot her a quizzical look.

"I can't believe that you want to continue with this charade now. Why in hell would you want to continue telling lies at this point? Why can't you simply tell the truth?"

Abby sat back down but continued. "All your appeals are exhausted, your execution date has been set...you have less than two months to live. Do you get that?" She was still yelling.

He tried to interrupt but she just shook her head and continued to talk. "As of this minute, we are through playing games. If you ever wanted anyone to know the truth, you better tell it today because this is our last meeting." Only then did Abby hush.

For the first time, the prisoner seemed at a loss for words. Up to this point, his stories seemed to be bringing him closer to answering the big questions. Still, Abby never knew, whether or not, she should believe him. His facts were sensational and shocking and they usually sounded made up. She always suspected he rehearsed for hours in his cell until it was performance perfect. Admittedly, she was often repulsed but equally intrigued by his vivid details. Still, she never knew how much of his oration to put her money on.

"I know you've been told this is our last visit."

Abby leaned across the table, wishing she could grab his lapel and shake the answers from him. Instead, she picked up her pen and notepad and waited. She was determined to write whatever the prisoner told her, word for word, and she prayed it would be the truth.

"I figured it would come soon. Your last visit, I mean." He threw his head back and looked up towards the tiny window. "What is it you want to know again?"

"Look, who you killed is a matter of public record. I just want you to fill in the blanks. I want to know the why. Why did you do it?" Abby waited for him to look at her again and added, with a tone of desperation in her voice, "And…who killed Jessie?"

The prisoner avoided eye contact. Abby wondered if she was losing him. His head sank lower, nearly touching the table. It was as though he could not bear to look up. Over the past few months, Abby never knew, at each visit, who she would encounter, what personality, or what range of emotions, he would present on the day. Prisoner #23897 was the identification stamped in indelible ink on his lapel. The identification number could just as easily stand for the total number of unpredictable personalities this man embodied.

Usually, his stereotypical convict persona was the first to greet her. Surly and vulgar, he would come on strong, a mad as hell, made-for-television intimidator. He was a bully, frightening until he tired of keeping up the charade. Then, he often turned childlike, playing with his chains, poking his fingers in and out of the links as though it was a toy. He cried a lot and pouted often, turning himself into the pitiful victim. Whether silly and joking, or sad and sullen, Abby never knew what to expect, so she just went with whatever personality she drew on the day. During the last few visits, he seemed to have softened a bit, dropping his tough-guy jailhouse image. Strange as it was, he had even started shaking Abby's hand at the end of each visit, just before the guard led him back to his cell. It was as though he was trying something new. Perhaps, just for her, he was trying to be a normal person, or spark a memory of the person he once was. The parting handshake always caught Abby off guard. It felt odd and creepy to touch the hand of someone she once thought she knew so well, especially, after finding out what those hands were capable of doing.

The prisoner's head and shoulders slumped over until his forehead rested on the table and stayed there for several seconds.

"Who killed Jessica Cline?" His voice boomed and his head shot up. "You have the nerve to ask *me* who killed her?" The prisoner's cuffed fists pounded the table and he looked ready to make a speech.

The tough-guy image had returned but his voice sounded deeper. He seemed to spit out the words that sounded darker and more dramatic than Abby had ever heard. He swallowed hard after each word and Abby feared he might hyperventilate at any moment.

"Every day," he gasped. "Every day Jessie spent at home, she was tortured." The prisoner swallowed and started to rock back and forth, as he spoke. "Mental abuse, beatings, other physical torture and rape — every day! And the very one who should have protected her, her father, was the biggest abuser of all...*Theo Cline!*" He pronounced the name and punctuated it with a mockingly thick, redneck twang.

Then he hushed and turned his gaze towards the ceiling. He began to tremble and as he fell back into the chair, Abby saw that his eyes had rolled up and back under his top eyelid so that all that was visible were the whites. He began to shake violently and make strange guttural sounds.

Should she call the guard? Was he having a seizure? Was he channeling the devil or was this just another attempt to manipulate the situation? Abby did not know but one thing was certain. At this moment, she was more afraid of him than ever.

She backed away from the white-eyed prisoner and slid, sideways along the wall, her back pressed against the cold cinderblocks, inching herself towards the door to call for help. She was within earshot of the guard and ready to call out but hesitated when she heard unusual sounds coming from the prisoner. He spoke in a foreign language, familiar, yet a language from some country she had never visited. She was sure she had heard that dialect before.

"Guard! GUARD! We're through in here!"

The door opened as the prisoner became completely uncontrollable and incoherent. As the guards led him away, the prisoner shouted and screamed intelligible words. She saw the warden come down the hall to meet her at the conference room door.

"Excuse me, Mrs. Wilcox. This is for you — we were afraid this might happen." The warden handed Abby an envelope, already opened and searched for contraband, of course.

"When the prisoner was told there would be no further visits allowed — standard procedure when a Death Warrant is issued, he asked that you get this." I'll give you a minute to read it before you leave but I'm sure you understand that all further visits with this prisoner are hereby suspended."

Abby sat alone in the conference room, reading the prisoner's words. It was a handwritten account of a dysfunctional childhood, which led to a merciless mental collapse. She read of the abuse he suffered at the hand of his own father. The beatings and atrocities he and his sister suffered were graphic and the details made Abby sick to her stomach.

The prisoner's words painted a clear picture. He explained how his sister's childhood mirrored the early life of Jessica Cline. Four years his junior, his sister, Kimberly endured incestuous abuse from the time she was a baby until her demise at age eight. Kimberly died at her own father's hand and the prisoner witnessed the murder.

"I was forced to watch my sister's abuse," he wrote, "until my father made me an accomplice. My job was to hold Kimberly down and cover her mouth so no one could hear her screams while my father forced himself on her."

Worse still, was the prisoner's recollection of his own arousal as he watched each instance of abuse. Clearly, he wrote, that made him just as guilty as his father. On the fateful day Kimberly died, his father pushed him aside and screamed, "Can't you do anything right?" Then he watched his father quiet Kimberly's sobs by holding a pillow over her mouth just a little too long.

His guilt lay dormant but never left him. Keeping that kind of secret consumed his formative years and hung in his psyche long after his father died. Every time he tried to save Kimberly — every time he tried to tell the awful story of what his father had done, his own guilt stopped him.

"From age twelve until sixteen, I was in a locked ward at Sheppard-Pratt Hospital in Maryland. At the time, our state had no ward for mentally ill teens so I was sent all the way from Georgia to Baltimore." The prisoner's letter had turned surprisingly personal and candid.

"By the time I was released, my father had committed suicide and my mother was, herself, emotionally incapacitated. A series of foster homes completed my upbringing and for the next few years, I put my childhood and my family behind me. I became normal, almost. I went to school, but for the wrong reasons. I fell in love and got married and that was for the right reasons but, then you know that, don't you, Abby?"

Abby gasped at seeing her name used with such bold familiarity and handwritten by a crazy man. The near-tenderness of the prisoner's words and the memories they stirred, tugged at her emotions. For a moment, Abby allowed herself to reminisce on her reasons for moving to North Carolina, the college classmate she thought she knew, the man who married her best friend.

Abby was startled back to reality by the sound of the opening door. She folded the letter, placed it inside her notebook and walked out of North Carolina Central Prison. She would finish reading the prisoner's words later, after she had left the prison grounds for what she now knew was the last time.

Safely off prison property, Abby pulled over at the first rest area she came across. Her curiosity about the remainder of the prisoner's words made it impossible for her to wait another minute to read it.

The letter continued. "I should have known the devil has no place in the pulpit but I tried to put myself there, anyway."

Abby remembered the prisoner's parting words before the guards took him away after he miraculously regained his ability to speak.

"You still don't understand why I had to do it?" He asked as the guards prepared to take him to back to his cell. "That's okay. You're a smart girl, Abby. You'll figure it out."

Then, while preparing to take him back to his cell, the guard pulled up the prisoner's sleeves for the routine contraband check before cuffing his wrists. She saw newly inked jailhouse tattoos on his arms, crudely applied but clear and legible. On his left arm, a red heart was split in half, the name," Jessie" on one side and "Kim" on the other. However, his right arm was what caught Abby's attention. She saw a heart, almost identical to the one on his left arm but bigger and it was covered with a name and surrounded by roses. Inked in elaborate calligraphy, it read, "Rachel".

That was when Abby remembered where she had heard the foreign language spewing from the prisoner's mouth. He was speaking in tongues — as he had always wanted to do. On their last night in the war room, she remembered his admission to James that he feared he would never be as good a preacher as his dad had been.

"My father was phenomenal...nearly as good as Billy Graham. He always told me what it took to be a great preacher. He said that speaking in tongues was a gift that only came to a chosen few — like him and Billy. He said a man knew he had the special calling to be a great preacher when speaking in tongues came naturally."

Abby remembered James' response to that statement. "But Tom, I don't think I ever heard Billy Graham speak in tongues." Tom did not seem to hear him.

It did not matter. Reverend Tom Kirby was certain that, one day, he would speak in tongues. Just like his father and Billy Graham. He was sure of it. Just as sure as he was that, he would get to heaven by punishing Jessica Cline's killer.

It was as though Jessica Cline's voice intertwined with Kimberly's and, the night of the fire, they became interchangeable. Had Tom taken on the task to avenge the death of both girls?

Later, sitting in her kitchen, Abby reread the letter to James. She told him about Tom speaking in tongues again.

Then she shared the prisoner's last words to her before they led him back to his cell.

"You asked me who killed Jessica Cline. Well, I don't know. At least, I don't know which of the Cline's actually held the knife that Halloween morning...and I don't care." His voice had returned to the almost normal, likeable man Abby once knew. "Important thing is...I got him...and now, Jessie can rest in peace."

Abby was upset. She folded the letter and ran to the bathroom so she could cry without the children seeing. It had been a stressful day.

After putting the kids to bed, James joined Abby back in the kitchen. He watched her work in silence, doing mundane chores, clearing dishes and wiping away the children's greasy handprints. He stopped her and took the dish sponge from her hands.

"Look at me," he said. "I want to tell you something before the kids interrupt us for a drink of water."

"I want to tell you how proud I am of you and I want you to know that I'm sorry we were never able to finished investigating Jessica Cline's murder. If we had, maybe all this would have turned out differently. But after you got hurt, it just wasn't worth it – you're too important." James hugged his wife.

"Most of all, though, I'm sorry you went through all that and never got answers." He hugged his wife and started out to answer the kids call for water. James stopped at the doorway and turned back to his wife.

"Why don't you go ahead and write that book anyway? Make up your own ending. Don't worry that he never confessed."

"Oh, but he did." Abby's voice was barely a whisper that she had not intended for James to hear. It was clear to her now. Tom had killed to avenge Jessica Cline's death. Now, she knew how he planned to avenge Kimberly's death. By gas chamber. Sins of the father...

Abby picked up the dish sponge to finish cleaning up little people smudges. She thought about her last visit to Central Prison and the revelation she had there.

She would not have to make up an ending. The ending was clear. It was the beginning – the beginning was wrong and perhaps, she had been concentrating on the wrong victim all along.

James stepped back into the kitchen. "What? Did I just hear you say he did tell you why?"

"Sort of. In his own, ecumenical way." Abby saw the confusion on James' face.

"Don't worry," she added. "It will all be in my book."

Maybe it's not about the happy ending. Maybe it's just about the story.

—*Abby Rials Wilcox*

For Robert, in appreciation for his lifelong work to right the wrongs, normalize the abnormal, protect those who deserve it, and detach himself from passive-aggression.

Acknowledgements

I wish to thank the following people for supporting me through this long journey to publication:

My Wilmington critique group, The Sea Quills, who suffered through the early drafts, giving their advice and encouragement as only those who have been there can provide. Especially, Bonnie Bunn Wyche, who taught us all to keep smiling and write until you draw your last breath.

The many friends and family who previewed early drafts then gave suggestions from a reader's perspective or just let me cry on their shoulders.

Those, living and dead, who inspired this story, especially the real Jessica Cline.

My children and grandchildren: Chris, Kevin, Jefferson, Lindsey N., Mary Carol, Lindsey P., Owen, McCartney, Claire, Lizzie, and Lewis. Each of you has either grown up in, married into, been born into, or were adopted by our crazy, wonderful family.

To my husband, Robert, a master gardener who knows the importance of pruning dead limbs and diseased roots to assure healthy growth, a tip that works great on family trees, too.